# ONE MAN BAND

By

Phil Pendleton

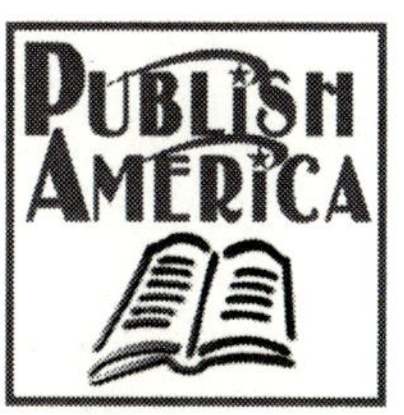


PublishAmerica
Baltimore

First printing

PublishAmerica has allowed this work to remain exactly as the author intended, verbatim, without editorial input.

Softcover 978-1-63084-115-7
PUBLISHED BY PUBLISHAMERICA, LLLP
www.publishamerica.com
Baltimore

Printed in the United States of America

# Foreword

> "Phillip was always a talker. This got him into trouble when he was in elementary school, but he soon learned when to talk and when to be quiet."

This was a quote from my dad, Steve Pendleton, in a book about me that my niece, Alexis, chose to put together as a class assignment in middle school. Little did I know then that "talking" would literally be my bread and butter, my career, and my chosen profession. In the same book my mother, Linda said...

*"Phillip...he is a gentle person. I know he liked to walk with God. He walked up the back yard on Clays Mill Road, where we lived, with a long stick pretending to be Moses when he was 5 years old. He loves people and makes everyone feel good. He will go far in life."*

Have I gone far in life? Yes I have. I have been blessed beyond measure, much like the line in the Michael English song titled, "In Christ Alone." This is a story about my life, my profession, and the people who have molded me. Everything that has happened to me has been for a reason. As my dad always says, "Everything happens for a reason" and "Everything will work out in the end."

The end hasn't happened for me yet. The road through this life I'm traveling is hopefully far from over, but the purpose of this book is show you a little bit of my journey, how I got here, and what I've learned. I hope you are encouraged, motivated, and challenged by what you're about to read.

So where do we begin?

How about from the beginning, where my life started. In Lexington, Kentucky.

# CHAPTER 1
## THE EARLY YEARS

I was born in Lexington, Kentucky at UK Hospital. It was 1970. I don't remember much about the first house we lived in, but most of my childhood years were spent at 3514 Clays Mill Road. I think I still remember my phone number there! It's amazing what you can remember when something is played over and over again. They say repetition is the best way to learn something. Maybe that's why I got into broadcasting. Because as a small kid...my parents say I would talk and talk. And talk some more.

In fact I remember in first grade talking so much my teacher, Mrs. Tandy, spanked me in the front of the whole class. Just for talking too much!

It was also at Stonewall Elementary that I first thought about journalism. Of course then I probably didn't even know what journalism was. But I knew about newspapers. Some mornings when I woke up before everyone else, I would go outside and get the newspaper.

I didn't read the sports section or the funny pages. No, I wanted to read about the day's events.

And then one day at school, I decided I wanted to write my own newspaper. But what was I going to write about? Well, what makes news today? Conflicts, crime, maybe a fight between people. Yeah, that makes the headlines and the 6 o'clock lead stories today.

Well, I remember there was a fight between two of the kids. And a girl won it by hitting a boy everyone knew was a bully. And the boy cried. Yes! That was a good story, so I wrote it. I got out some notebook paper and put it all into print.

When I got home that night, I showed my parents my finished product. I knew they were impressed because it made them laugh. No, they weren't laughing at me. They were laughing because they were proud of my accomplishments.

That was probably about the 3rd or 4th grade. But it wasn't until junior high that I had my first real clue that something called "*broadcasting*" would be my career path.

# CHAPTER 2
## WINNING THE SPEECH TEAM EVENT

It was 1983 and I was 13. I was in the 8th grade at Jessie M. Clark Junior High. I was never an athletic person so most of the extracurricular activities like soccer, basketball, football or baseball were not for me. Plus, I really never had a liking for sports as a youngster.

But there was a group called the Speech Team. Wow, a team for talking! A competition for running your mouth. Now, that's the ticket! A club you can be a part of just for doing the one thing you love, and that you usually get in trouble for. Wow, Mom and Dad will sure be proud of me!

So I joined up. There were no tryouts, no competition for the lead roles, anyone could be a part of the speech team. So I joined. The next question was "What category do you want?"

"Drama?"

"Prose?"

"Poetry?"

No, no to all of that.

"Broadcasting?"

What was that?

"Broadcasting. Well, that's when you give the news."

Give the news. Now that sounds exciting. Yes, that is what I want. That decision started a long journey that I am still fortunate to be a part of. And here's how it started.

The speech team was like a lot of other sports teams. You practice. But instead of lifting weights, running around the track or tackling and shooting drills, you read your copy over and over again until you read it correctly and clearly.

So much of my practice involved reading old Associated Press copy over and over again. It wasn't easy because many of the words were places and names hard to pronounce, such as leaders of foreign countries in international stories.

After weeks of practice it was time for our first "meet." I was an 8th grader, I was put on the "B team," as the "A team" was reserved for the 9th graders.

I went to school early that Saturday morning and was given several copies of news stories that I had very little time to read over. Probably like 10 minutes. I was supposed to put the stories in the proper order, meaning the most important or "lead" stories were first followed by the next important ones, then features, and them some "fluff" pieces. The judges would grade us not just on how well we read the stories but by the order of events.

I remember my judge was the news director of WVLK Radio. After I had my news copy together and when my name was called, I went into a small room, with just a small desk and two chairs. Mr. Riggens sat on one side of the desk, I was on the other facing him. He had a stop watch to time me and I had my copy in front of me. He was to judge me on how well I read the story, how I pronounced and enunciated the copy.

I'll be honest. I didn't think I did very well. My copy had a lot of names I didn't know how to pronounce and the content was difficult to understand. But I finished, handed him the copy and went on to wait for the results.

At the end of the day, an awards ceremony was held to hand out trophies for first, second and third place honors for the winners in each speech event. I sat in the hard bleachers of the Jessie Clark gym waiting for the awards, thinking,

"*There's no way I'm winning anything today. That copy was just too hard to read, to understand, to comprehend. What a waste this has been.*"

But I was wrong. Very wrong.

As they were announcing the broadcasting awards, I heard,

"And first place for the broadcasting competition....in the B-Team category.....Phillip Pendleton!"

What, had they just called my name? Was there a mistake? Surely I didn't really win?

But I had! I ran down the bleachers to the cheering crowd and got my trophy. First place in broadcasting. I was so proud.

I remember that my parents didn't attend the awards ceremony but as they were picking me up I recall *running* to their car, jumping into the back seat and proudly holding out my new prized possession, a bright gold (it was actually just plastic) trophy. "I won! I won! First place in broadcasting."

And it was the next thing I said that would mold me for the rest of my life.

"Now I know what I want to do for my career. I want to go into broadcasting!"

# CHAPTER 3
## FROM BOY SCOUTS TO YOUTH GROUP

Now let me rewind a bit. Let's go back a little to elementary school because I need to tell a little more about another important event in my life. How I became a Christian.

I wasn't one of the popular kids in school. I really never had a lot of friends. I did have one good friend in elementary school. His name was Alan. But as the years went on...Alan would get new friends and I would just, well, exist you could say. Sure, I had some guys I liked to hang out with, but never established a close bond with a lot of people.

Like back then, and probably today, the kids that don't have a lot of friends are often the ones who get 'picked on' by others. And I was no different.

I will never forget one day at lunch when a group sitting across from me started the insults. I don't remember what they said. But it was my response that I remember vividly.

I remember looking up at the sky, as if looking at God Himself, and asking "why? Why do you let me go through this. Why are they doing this me? Why are they making me feel so bad?"

The kids just looked at me as if I had lost my mind. But later on I would use that moment to share my testimony with others. A testimony given at Asbury College during a youth event that saw several kids give their lives to Jesus.

The Bible says "Suffering produces perseverance, perseverance, character and character hope. And hope does not disappoint." (NIV.)

I believe God let me go through that suffering so that I could help others as a teenager who had been bullied in school. But I wouldn't realize that gift until much later.

As someone who wanted to belong to a group, an organization, and partly because my brother, Todd, was involved, I joined the Boy Scouts in 6th grade.

The troop I was in had a very convenient location in that it was in a church right next door to the house I lived in. I could walk to the Monday night meetings. We did a lot of the things many other boy scouts did such as camping, jamborees, and events to earn merit badges.

I started out as a Tenderfoot, and made it all the way to a Life scout. But I learned by the time I was 14 or 15 that scouting was not for me. Some of the kids in my troop seemed to have this "I'm better than everyone else" mentality so I quickly decided to leave and not go back. It was about this time that I noticed the youth group at my church was doing many of the same kind of events.

My brother and I had been going to Park United Methodist Church because that's where my grandparents attended when they lived in Lexington. But when Todd went off to college, I didn't have a ride. That's when Mark Walz became not just my youth minister, but also a very dear friend.

Mark lived close by and it wasn't out of his way to swing by my house on Sunday mornings and pick me up and take me to church. It wasn't long before I saw that going to scouting events and taking part in youth group activities were going to conflict so I quit the scout troop and got more involved in church. And I still believe that was a wonderful decision.

Unlike most "Christians," I don't remember the exact moment I became a Christian. Many will tell you of a salvation moment when they heard a preacher give a sermon and then, full of emotion they will come forward, announce a decision to follow God and get baptized.

But during a week in Summer camp or Youth Discipleship Retreat in Barbourville at Union College I remember hearing a youth minister talk about living for God and I remember knowing then that I need a closer relationship with God. I remember crying and feeling very close to God.

After that I attended church every Sunday. I went to "youth group" every Sunday night. And every summer I went to Youth Discipleship Retreat. I met a lot of friends that I still have to this day.

Mark Walz has since passed away of cancer but Mark had an incredible influence on me. I think what I enjoyed most about Mark was that he lived life to the fullest and showed me that being a Christian didn't mean that you could not have fun.

"Jesus had fun," he would say. "In fact I think Jesus had more fun than anyone else then!"

Mark showed me that you can have incredible joy in this life. And what a jokester he was. Always pulling practical jokes on people. Like walking up to a stranger, handing them some deodorant and saying, "Here, buddy, you need this more than I do."

Or having us all go to a crowded store and walk through it wearing scuba gear! Or collectively lying down in a mall and waving our hands and feet in the air yelling, "I'm a dead bug! I'm a dead bug!"

But Mark was also a very gentle, loving, kind person. He put others before him and would go out of his way to make sure those he cared about were taken care of.

The world lost a great soul when he passed away in 2010. But his legacy lives on in his children and in me.

In fact before he was married and before he had children, Mark told me, “Phillip, if I ever have a son, I hope he’s like you.”

Wow, what a compliment.

So, my teenage years were filled with becoming a God follower and realizing that I wanted a career in broadcasting.

# CHAPTER 4
## COLLEGE

I went to Eastern Kentucky University. Why? Well, my brother went there, it was close to home but far enough away to require me to live in a dorm and because I had heard it had a good broadcasting program. But for me, I wanted a career in radio. And not just any radio- Christian radio. I actually had wanted to attend a Christian university, but most religious schools were private and too expensive. So I settled on Eastern. It was a good choice, though, because a lot of my friends from high school were going there and one of them was even going to be my roommate.

I settled into college rather easily, but having come from a good youth group I quickly felt out of place. I longed for the fellowship and friends that my youth group had offered me. Eastern had a lot of good Christian organizations: the Methodist Wesley Home, Christian Student Fellowship, and the Baptist Student Union.

Because I grew up in the Methodist church, I settled into the Wesley Foundation. The organization had a small but loyal group of followers but I had a difficult time "fitting in," so eventually I got involved with the Christian Student Fellowship and Baptist Student Union. The "BSU" had weekly worship services, and a lot of fun fellowship events. It was there that I met many of the friends that I have today, including my wife, my best friend of all. But most importantly, the "B" as we called it, offered a retreat of sorts, a solace from the stresses of college cramming, and a place where friends could lean on each other.

But college was about getting an education and preparing for your future career and it was there that I received my preparation for what would at first be a career in radio and later in television news. The first two years were about taking the basic courses mixed with a general course in journalism, the history of broadcasting, etc. Classes to make sure you are a "well rounded" person. Whatever that means!

To be truthful I'm not sure that much of what I learned in the college classroom prepared me for the jobs that I had but you can't get a good job without a degree and coursework is required. As I said before, I wanted to get a job in radio. specifically Christian radio. But you couldn't just take coursework in radio. You had to take classes that prepared you for *broadcasting*.

One of my first classes taught me how to write news copy. The professor in that class, Marie Mitchell, who was also the News Director of the campus public radio station, noticed something about my writing that led her to offer me a part time job at the station. I was actually surprised by this because in one of my first assignments, she marked up my paper with so much red ink that I could barely see what I had written to begin with! Still, her attention not only gave me a job with some additional income, it showed me that a career in news was a real possibility.

# CHAPTER 5
## THE REAL WORLD

In the summer of 1992 I was a college graduate looking for work. With no solid job leads I armed myself with a handful of resumes and took to the streets. I was still living in Richmond, Kentucky, so I decided I would drive a 50-mile radius around Richmond in hopes of finding a job at a radio station. I went to Lexington, Winchester, Danville and a few other towns. But it was in Danville were I found gold. Or at least $5.50 an hour!

The day after I left a resume at WHIR/WMGE I got a call from Brian Conn. He was the program director/morning announcer at the combo in Danville. A "combo' is basically how you described a station that had both an "AM" and an "FM" station. He was impressed that I was looking for a job and with my college degree and the resume.

"Now I can't promise you anything full-time, I only need someone working about 30 hours a week, at night," he told me.

"That's OK. It's a start. It's all I am looking for right now," I said.

So that's how my post-college broadcasting career started. It was a job. No benefits. A small paycheck. But it was something.

I was still living in Richmond and because the job was only part time and during the evening, I knew I would need more income. So I kept my fast-food job in the morning in Richmond, then drove to Danville for the evening shift radio job. I was basically working form 11 a.m. to 3 p.m. in the morning-afternoon, then driving to Danville for a 3 p.m. to 9 p.m. shift. It was a long day but I WAS WORKING IN RADIO!

The job at WHIR was basically as a utility player at first. I would write news and sports copy, deliver a short news and sports cast on the "afternoon drive" shift, then I would record and edit commercials for the morning shows the next day. It wasn't much but I knew I was gaining valuable experience that I would use in full time jobs down the road.

Eventually the part-time job at WHIR/WMGE turned into a full-time position as the station hired me to be their mid-morning announcer and newscaster. I was able to move to Danville and quit my fast-food job in Richmond. The pay was still $5.50 an hour and although it was 40 hours a week it still wasn't really enough to live on. But there was a small apartment above the station that my boss let me move into until I could find a more permanent place to live. Not having to pay rent was probably worth about a $200 to $300 monthly savings so it was an ideal situation.

As they say, all good things come to an end and soon the station hired a new sales manager who needed the upstairs for his office so I needed to find a new place to live. I was devastated at first, because I had no idea where I would go. Where was I going to find a new, free place to live? Or was I going to have to find a part-time job?

I've always believed that God will always provide. I prayed and He answered. In the form of a log cabin!

That's right. A log cabin literally became my home. I don't remember how I found the place. It could have been an ad in the paper or something I saw at the station, but a couple in Danville was looking for someone to stay in a one room efficiency apartment and basically do work for them on their property. It was simple. Work for the landlord and live for free? That was minus $25 a month for utilities and water. What a deal! And the "apartment" I lived in was a log cabin behind the home the landlords lived in.

They told me that I could either pay $200 a month in rent or work so many hours a week mowing the grass, painting, and basically keeping up the property. From the outside the apartment looked like a historic log cabin, but the inside was modern with a kitchen, bathroom, and a living room and bedroom combination. It was small, but perfect, just what I needed. And it would be my home until I got married.

# CHAPTER 6
## TROUBLES WITH RADIO

My experiences with radio have been much the same with just about every station I have worked at. Money is tight and when there isn't enough, your pay gets cut, payroll can't be met, or at the worst, people lose their jobs. Those situations have happened at every station I have worked at.

I must say I give Brian Conn a lot of credit because he took a real gamble with me and I found out later that the owners really didn't want to hire me because they didn't think they could afford another employee. And about a year into my stint there I realized just how bad things were. I'm not really sure why things were bad. Maybe it was mis-management, poor decisions or whatever but sometime around late 1993 into early 1994, we were all told that our health insurance was being cut and we were going to lose 5% of our salaries because of the station's financial problems. I ended up making up the difference by getting a part-time job at a local grocery store but I saw the storm coming and knew I needed to get out.

### LONDON, Ky.

In the spring of 1994 I started looking for another job and I found it in London, Ky. The station was looking for a news director and they hired me after the first interview. The pay was a little better than what I was making in Danville but it was enough that I wouldn't need to work two jobs.

A lot happened in June 1994. I quit my job at WHIR, got married several days later and went on our honeymoon to Myrtle Beach. Then the Monday after we got back I hopped in my car at 4 a.m., and drove the hour drive to London for my first day at WFTG radio.

My job at WFTG included delivering four or five morning newscasts and then spending the next several hours of the day gathering stories. I would do several interviews over the phone with local officials, police contacts and community folk. Then several nights a week I was required to cover the local city council, school board or county fiscal court meetings. The days were long but I didn't mind because I had my first full-time job. When I look back, I think the pay wasn't great but to me it was plenty. The problem was the station owners didn't like the fact that I was driving so far from Stanford to London every day and they wanted me to live closer. My problem was my wife and I had just bought a house in Stanford and she was able to land a job teaching school in Stanford and I didn't want her to have to drive a long way every day.

So the compromise was that we would rent a small apartment in Mt. Vernon, half-way between London and Stanford. We would keep our house and possibly rent it to someone else. But just before we were about to move, God answered a big prayer and we didn't have to move.

## WRSL

I remember the phone call like it happened yesterday. I was on my couch watching TV, probably thinking or worrying about having to move to Mt. Vernon. The call was from the former sales manager at WHIR/WMGE, you know the one whose office required me to move out of the upstairs apartment? Ironic, because that phone call from him was the start of the process that kept me in Stanford and put a stop to the move that would put us out of our house and into a tiny Mt. Vernon apartment.

The sales manager was Norb King. Norb and his family moved to Kentucky from Iowa for the Danville station job and he left the station for the same reasons I did. I think he ended up in Richmond but didn't stay there long. That's because he accepted an offer to manage WRSL in Stanford, where he was living, too, by the way. The call from him was to offer me a job being news director of WRSL. He knew I was driving back and forth to London every day and might be interested in working closer to home. And closer it was! It was less than a mile away.

So long story short, I interviewed for the job and accepted it. I still remember pulling into the driveway, getting out of the car and running up to my wife, yelling "We're staying here! I got the job!" The job in Stanford would mean that we wouldn't have to move, and I would no longer be driving an hour one-way to go to work. It seemed to be perfect. My wife and I were both employed with full time jobs and our jobs and home were in the same town.

WRSL had not had a full-time news director before. And people in the town were not used to a radio news person calling them for interviews. I was met with a lot of skepticism and some of the people didn't take me real seriously....at first.

WRSL 95.9 FM was a true small town station. All the announcers were local and the station "signed off" at midnight. That means the station didn't broadcast anything from midnight to 6 a.m. But when announcer Arvil "Plow" Jones signed on in the mornings..the first thing that aired was my 6 a.m. newscast. I had newscasts again at 7, 8, and 10 a.m.

Then I would record a newscast for noon, and 4,5, and 6 p.m. For the next seven years my job there was much the same. I was delivering newscasts in the morning, gathering news in the morning and afternoons and covering city council and school board meetings at night. The days were long but just having a job close to home made it all worth it.

WRSL was owned by Lincoln-Garrard Broadcasting Company and its president was an attorney who grew up in Lincoln County but lives and works in Chicago. Jonathan Smith is also the son of the station's original owner. He had a lot of hopes and dreams for WRSL and although it was a "small town" station, he wanted it to be a lot more than what it was. He hired Norb as general manager, me as news director but later he and Norb were able to find some pretty talented announcers and "dee-jays" that established a very respected station. Later, the frequency changed to 96.3 FM and Jon was able to boost the power. When WRSL was 95.9 FM I think the station only reached around Stanford to part of Lancaster and really didn't cover all of Lincoln County. But they moved the tower and with 25,000 watts they were able to cover a good chunk of central Kentucky.

The station was growing and garnering more listeners. In addition to doing the news I was also responsible for sports coverage.

When I grew up in Lexington, Ky. I was never a big fan of sports. I liked Kentucky basketball but usually when my dad had a ball game on, if it was something other than Kentucky basketball I wasn't that interested. But that all changed when I started covering sports in radio. I became the "sideline reporter" for the local high school football team, meaning at certain moments in the game, I would deliver short highlights or call PATs, point after touchdown extra points. Later I would call play-by-play and it was during this time I developed a love for football and other sports.

When I worked for WRSL radio and living in Stanford, I figured it could easily be the radio job that I retired from. My employer was giving me good raises and while the money wasn't outstanding, it was enough. Plus, my wife had a good job teaching school and both of our jobs were stable. But deep inside there was a longing to do something more and there was something about television news that really started peaking my interest.

I think it was watching how the Lexington stations covered the Kentucky basketball teams in the mid-late 1990's that really influenced me to explore a possible career in broadcast television.

From about 1995 to 1998, every spring the Lexington TV stations went all out in following the UK teams wherever they went when it came to basketball tournament time. Whether it was the SEC tournaments or NCAA's, wherever Kentucky was playing, the TV news and sports crews followed. I knew those reporters were working but it looked like so much fun. I was thinking, 'if I could get a job in TV news,' I would have the possibility of covering the UK team and or its fans.. whether it be in Dallas, Atlanta, New Orleans or wherever. That would be the best of both worlds. You would be working, but you would be traveling as well.

The problem was that other than classes I had in college, I didn't have an ounce of television experience. Who would hire me?

It was about this time that I received a phone call from Bill Bryant, the current WKYT noon and 5:30 p.m. news anchor, at WKYT-TV, the CBS affiliate in Lexington. He was looking for some information about a "snake handler" bitten during a church service in Garrard County. He knew about my work as news director covering that area and thought I was probably working on the same story. After talking to him for a few minutes I went outside and got in the radio station van, in attempts to find this church. I never did find it but when I called Bill back, the conversation was the starting point in helping me find something much more valuable: a career in TV news. But it wouldn't happen for several more years. The conversation went something like this:

"Bill, I know you have a background in radio, I was just wondering, do you all ever hire people from radio backgrounds in television anymore?" I asked.

"It can happen, but mostly we hire people with television experience. But if you are interested, I will keep you in mind, if we have something I think you might be qualified for," he said.

We talked longer but the weeks turned into months and years and when I didn't hear back from him and saw other reporters receive jobs, I figured my chances of getting hired in television were slim to none. As you'll read later, my chance to work in television actually came when I really didn't want it anymore!

# CHAPTER 7
## MORE TOUGH TIMES IN RADIO

In 2000, Norb King decided he had enough of the rat race and got out of radio, with Jonathan Smith promoting me to general manager. It would prove to be much more than I could handle. I basically took on both roles of news director and general manager. In the beginning, it was great. I was fairly successful in leading both departments but after nine months the stress was just too much to handle. It was during this time that I learned of an opening at WVLK AM 590 in Lexington as just a news announcer. The job would be half the stress but a lot less pay as well. In the end I decided that I would take the less stress and less pay combo. I started working for the Lexington station in November of 2001.

The irony of what happened is very interesting. I said earlier that when I was in high school I dreamed of one day working in Christian radio. I love Christian rock music and had hoped to one day to spin tunes by the likes of White Heart, Petra, Stryper or Rez Band and give testimonials in between songs. The problem was that Christian radio was almost nonexistent in central Kentucky.

About the same time I was considering a career change, Jonathan Smith was also considering a change in his radio station ownership. He had received an offer from the company that owns the K-Love and Air-One Christian stations. They wanted to use the WRSL 96.3 FM frequency so he and that organization worked out an agreement to bring listener-supported, Christian music radio to central Kentucky. I don't know if my leaving to work at WVLK had a direct result in the new Christian radio station or not, but the timing is very interesting. Basically, I had to leave to have the station that I wanted! Talk about irony.

I enjoyed working for WVLK but I must say, working in a larger radio market is much more structured and strict than small town radio. There are formats and specific rules to follow and you have to say things nearly exactly how the program director wants you to say them. But it was also a busy time because my employment began a few months after the 9/11 terrorist attacks and there was a lot more news both on the local and national levels.

My day began with an hour or so drive to Lexington then a cup of coffee, news writing, telephone interviews, and usually hour and half-hour newscasts between 10 a.m. and 6 p.m. Since I was required to write and deliver so many newscasts, nearly all of our content was produced in-house with nearly all of our interviews done over the phone or from field stories our TV partner WTVQ helped us with.

So I was back to driving a long distance back and forth to work. But the good thing was that I didn't have the responsibility of managing a station in addition to producing news content. But after a while I decided that it was time to do something else and that's when I found a career writing for a newspaper.

# CHAPTER 8
## THE ADVOCATE MESSENGER

In the summer of 2003, I received a job offer from The Advocate Messenger in Danville, Ky. The position was writing Garrard County news content and since we lived in Lancaster, the Garrard county seat, it was essentially a job working from home. They suited me up with a laptop computer with a high speed internet connection and the only time I had to actually go the newspaper office was to attend trainings, staff meetings or the occasional Danville assignment. And since my home was considered "my office" I was reimbursed mileage for whenever I drove from the house to an assignment. It was terrific. I would get up in the mornings about 7:30 or 8 a.m., make a few phone calls, drive to the courthouse, city hall, or some "news event" cover it, and then come back home and put it together on the laptop. The "lunch hour" was essentially me in front of the TV with a plate of food for 45 minutes to an hour. Since most of my evenings were spent covering meetings, I caught up on my favorite shows or DVD's during my lunch hours.

My daughter, who was 4 at the time, loved it because usually by the time she got home from preschool I was ready for a "break" so I would spend my "breaks" playing with her. Break time became Barbie time, or in my case, time to be "the prince." It was the ideal situation and it was fantastic for the family. The only down side was having to work a lot of late nights covering city council or school board meetings but usually they let me make that up by getting off early or taking days off. But in the event there was a lot going on they simply paid me overtime. Mileage reimbursements and overtime were used as extra money or "Christmas" money. I thought, "Wow this is a job I know I hold for a long, long time." And that's when I got the phone call from WKYT that changed everything.

# CHAPTER 9
## Time for TV

It doesn't say this in the Bible but it seems like a verse that *should be* in there. "Don't get too comfortable in anything, because just when you do, it will change." I loved my job as a staff writer for the Advocate-Messenger.

And one thing about it that I didn't mention above was that small town or medium sized newspapers, unlike broadcast radio or television, do not limit you on when you can take vacation or days off. Let me explain. Most radio and television stations measure their audience viewing or listening habits so they can tell their advertisers who is watching or listening and when. In the business, we call it ratings. In both radio and TV there are certain times of the year, usually in month-long increments, when these ratings are taken. In both mediums, employees are prohibited from taking off so that each station's full staffs are available. When I worked for WVLK I wasn't allowed to take off when listeners kept their diaries or ratings books. At the Advocate, there is no such ratings period, so I could take off pretty much whenever I wanted. That was another blessing, another one that I would be giving up in going back into the broadcast business.

Like I said above, everything was wonderful when I got the phone call that I will never forget. Remember me talking about the conversation with me asking anchor Bill Bryant if they "ever hired anyone out of radio?" And how when the months turned into years without a follow up call I figured that conversation was basically a waste of time? Well, it wasn't a waste. And Bill didn't forget about me. Not for a long shot.

When we lived in Lancaster we got an unlisted number because of some prank phone calls and because I worked for the news media. So I'm not sure how Bill got my phone number but I will never forget coming home one day and having the following conversation with my wife.

"You're never going to believe who left a message for you," she said.

"Who?" I asked.

"Just listen," she said and played the answering machine.

"Yes, Phil this is Bill Bryant with 27 Newsfirst. Listen, there is something I need to talk to you about. Please call me at your earliest convenience."

Wow. That's all I could say. What did he want? Like most of the news anchors at all the Lexington TV stations, Bill had somewhat of a "celebrity" aura about him and just getting a message from him was an honor. I figured he probably wanted to ask me about a story I had written for The Advocate since the Lexington news station considered the paper a source. So I called him.

The conversation got right to the purpose of his call.

"Phil, listen, we are looking for someone for our southern Kentucky bureau that is based in Somerset. I know you live in Lancaster but you're still a lot closer to Somerset (about 45 minutes) than we are and I was wondering if you would by chance be interested."

To be honest, it was a phone call I wished I had received about 3 years earlier, but the fact that they were considering me about knocked my socks off. But the truth of the matter was that I truly loved working from home and writing for the small town newspaper. I wasn't making a ton of money but the overtime and mileage reimbursements were actually a lot more than I first thought they would be.

But to work in TV? Other than college I had no television experience but Bill saw something in me that probably few others would. He said people who work in radio have an understanding of hard work, deadlines and telling stories with words that even some people who have worked in TV alone for decades never grasp. He strongly encouraged me to apply for job, even if I thought I might not be interested.

So I did. The position was very unique because while it was a job working for WKYT, the "Southern Kentucky Bureau" position was actually shared with three other stations. The position was based at The Center for Rural Development, a large building in Somerset that is part convention center/office building/telecommunications facility. The other stations I would technically work for were WYMT 57 Mountain News in Hazard, WBKO in Bowling Green and WVLT TV in Knoxville, Tenn.

The Center had the capabilities through high speed internet to "feed" stories to all 4 stations and because Somerset was geographically in the middle of the four TV market, it made since for a reporter to feed stories in that area to all four stations.

The position was also a "one man band," meaning that the reporter was also the videographer and editor. You did everything by yourself. You shot your story, then you wrote, voiced and edited it.

Bill told me a little about the position but he said that Steve Crabtree, who once held the same position years ago and was then the news director at WVLT, would actually interview for the position. Steve wanted ownership over the new hire because he was from the area and knew "what it took."

But I still wasn't sold on the position. I knew it really wouldn't pay me much more than I was making at the newspaper and I would have to drive to Somerset every day. It would be more time away from home for not a whole lot more money. But I agreed to the interview.

Steve interviewed me at the bureau for two hours. He did a really good job of laying out the pros and cons and after the interview I did believe there were more pros. But I still didn't think I would take the position.

But what happened next is a true example of what has happened several times in my life. I am firm believer in the bible verse, "Seek ye first the Kingdom of God and his righteousness, and all these things will be added onto you as well." Matthew 6:33, NIV. Numerous times in my life I have received what I wanted when I really didn't want it anymore.

And that's how my first TV job started. When I stopped looking for the big time broadcast gig, it came calling. When I didn't want it anymore.

Steve told me after the interview to think about things for several days and he would call me. Or for me to call him back. I don't remember which. For regardless of who called who, it was the phone call that I received right before that changed my destiny...possibly forever.

# CHAPTER 10
## A GRANDFATHER'S ADVICE

Two people that I loved and respected all my life were my grandmother and father Pendleton. I called them Grandmama and Grandaddy. Yeah, I know that sound juvenile but I just never stopped calling them by what my older brother and I started calling them as little children.

When I was very little, about 5, my parents went through a divorce and my brother, then 11, and I and went out to Phoenix, Arizona to stay with my grandparents while the divorce was being finalized. I more or less went to kindergarten in Arizona and my brother Todd attended most of his 5$^{th}$ grade there. My grandparents, despite living more than a thousand miles away, were extremely influential on my life and more importantly, my faith.

When I was about 10 or 11, my grandparents during a trip to see us in Lexington took my brother and me to church and from that time on Todd and I kept going even when my parents did not. Later, my youth minister, Mark Walz, picked up when my brother went off to college.

Grandmama and Grandaddy were great advice givers and they always seemed to have that special kind of wisdom you can only receive from the older generation. I'll never forget my grandfather once getting out a register he kept of every tithe he gave to his church.

"I've always given 10% and I've never gone without," he would say.

Well, back to the TV job offer. Right before I was to make my decision to "take it or leave it," I got a phone call from my grandfather. It was unusual because whenever my grandparents called, you didn't just talk to one of them. You talked to both. They always had their two recliners, each with their own remote control (to the same TV) and two cordless phones. So when you talked to them, they were both on the phone. But this time it was different. Grandaddy was the only one I remember talking to that day.

"Whatcha doing.....Phillip!" he said.

"Well, it's funny you called. I'm actually considering a job change."

"Really? Doing what?"

"Well, I don't think I'm going to do it, but a TV station is offering me a job being a reporter, but I really like working from home and spending time with my family so I think I'm going to turn them down," I said.

I thought my grandfather would side with me here because it was one thing my grandfather was...as a great family man. My grandparents stayed committed to each other for more than 60 years. They were as tight as a couple as couples get and they loved each other and valued their family greatly.

But my grandfather's response surprised me.

"You mean to tell me you have a *TELEVISION STATION* offering you a job and you're about to turn them down?!!" he exclaimed.

"Well, yes, because like I said...I'm working from home and spending time with my family...and..."

"But it is a TV job! Those don't come calling often, I assume," he said.

"Yeah....you're right," I agreed. I had waited years for this opportunity and here I was about to tell them to look for someone else.

"Phillip, I trust you'll do the right thing but don't turn them down so quickly. Think about this. Think about the opportunity this will mean for your family. Think about the size of the station compared to the size of the paper you're working for. What this could mean down the road," he said.

We talked a while longer and by the time I hung up I had changed my mind. After thinking about it, praying about it and talking about with Allissa, I made the decision to jump into the work of television news.

# CHAPTER 11
## TRAINING FOR TV

So I put my two weeks' notice into The Advocate-Messenger and prepared for what would be the biggest job change I would ever make. Working for WKYT-TV and its parent company, Gray Television would clearly be the largest company I had ever worked for and obviously the most prestigious. But first I had to learn how to do just about everything.

When I was in college I had a few broadcasting television classes but honestly I didn't' take them that seriously and did just enough to get by because I really didn't think I would ever need anything I learned in them. I was going to be a radio man! I didn't need to learn how to edit video!

Boy was I wrong. But what happened next was essentially learning in a month what I should have learned over several years in college. I needed to learn how to professionally shoot video with what is called an ENG (Electronic News Gathering) camera and I needed to learn how to edit video.

Shooting video didn't really seem like much of a challenge because I had used a camcorder ever since my first child was born, but there was a lot more to it than just hitting play and record looking through a viewfinder. You had to shoot in such a way to tell a story in pictures and to make shots look good that when editing, the stories would flow and make sense. But what really scared me was whether I would be able to learn how to edit.

In college I remember trying to edit a few stories without even knowing how to do it. I since learned that I was doing it backwards then. While I was going through training, I asked one of the shooters if he could explain in simplest terms how to edit.

"You worked in radio, right?," he asked.

"Yeah, for like 8 years," I said.

"Well, when you put down your audio tracks, you would edit your voice tracks then your sound bites, right?" he asked.

The "voice tracks" are when I do the talking, the "sound bites" are the segments of the person being interviewed that make the news story.

"Yeah, that's pretty much it," I agreed.

"In TV, all you're doing is laying down your voice tracks, then your sound bites, and then you put pictures, or video, overtop the voice tracks that make the news story makes sense," he said.

He had just explained in one sentence that for whatever reason I never grasped in two or three years in college. The problem was just doing it. I admit, it took me two hours to edit my first package. Now I can edit a story in 20 minutes or less.

I was hired at WKYT in late October 2003 and started the first week of November. But I didn't start actually reporting the news until early December. The first month or so was spent shadowing, training, and basically learning how to be a "one man band."

Honestly, the first several days at WKYT were spent observing some and standing around a lot. It's hard for someone to train you in a job when they have a job to do themselves. I remember riding around with our chief photographer and whatever reporter he was with that day. I spent several days learning the "lingo" of broadcasting. For example, before TV,

I had no idea what the different between a "package" or a "VOSOT" was. Or what "B-roll" meant.

A "package" is at 1 to 2 minute story that usually the reporter puts together or "voices." Sometimes it begins and ends with a "stand up" where you see the reporter begin and end the story and in the middle of the piece you hear the reporter's voice in between sound bite segments of the person being interviewed. A "VOSOT" is an acronym for "voice over, sound on tape" and generally it's where the anchor reads broadcast copy and you see video of a story with a sound-bite near the middle or end. A "VO" or voice over is simply the anchor reading over news copy.

I remember feeling very overwhelmed at first. There was so much to learn and so many things I had never done before. Learning how to use the big "ENG" or "Electronic News Gathering" camera was difficult as well, because not only was it heavy, it had more switches than anything I had every used before. Plus, there's an art, a technique to using it. You can't just point and shoot. We're told to shoot frames of 15 seconds each of wide, medium and tight shots so that you can have a sequence of shots to edit together that will make sense in a story.

## Disappointment

The first story I shot and edited was the day before Thanksgiving, 2003. I was still technically in training and I wasn't on the list of approved stories so my assignment was basically just busy work. I didn't know if it would make the air or not, and the management at the story wasn't really sold on my work just yet. But I was eager to learn and get to work so I embarked on my assignment.

The story was pretty simple. The mall and stores getting ready for the big Black Friday sales the Wednesday before Thanksgiving. I went out to several stores and Fayette Mall and interviewed manager and shoppers getting ready for the kickoff of the busy Christmas shopping season. It took almost all day to get all the footage and then editing took at least 2 more hours. At the end of the day, there wasn't room for the story on WKYT's 5 or 6 p.m. newscasts but I was told the story would air on the Fox 56 10 O'clock News..which WKYT helped produce. Wow! My first story on the news and I WOULD BE ON THE NEWS! I was so excited I called everyone in my family and told them to watch the Fox news that night.

At 10 p.m. that Wednesday night, I sat in the front of the TV waiting for my big debut. The first 10 minutes is usually the news segment and it came and went with no story. I wasn't too worried because another 10 minute segment would air at 10:30. But 10:40 came and went and no story. All that work. All that labor. All that time for nothing, I thought. I was extremely disappointed.

And then the next day we went to my parent's house and had to explain to grandparents, aunts, uncles and cousins why I wasn't on the news. And trying to explain my new job to them was difficult.

"So are you a reporter or a camera man?" they would ask.

"Well, it's kinda both," I would say.

"What?" they would say.

I admit it *is* confusing. I still get asked by people "Where's your cameraman?" Or

"You mean they haven't promoted you to having a camera man yet?"

I realize most people are used to seeing the camera man and reporter "crew" and find it strange when they see someone talking into a camera by themselves. When I first started I was actually only one of two "one man bands" or "multi-media journalists" at WKYT but WYMT in Hazard and WBKO in Bowling Green had several. In fact, many of the smaller market TV stations exclusively use one man bands. But larger markets initially shied away from them, I think mainly because many live TV situations require a photographer to also operate a LIVE truck.

So Thanksgiving weekend came and went with me wondering when I would finally prove to everyone in my family that I was REALLY a TV reporter. As it turns out, my first TV package would not air for several more weeks.

The first week after Thanksgiving involved me working in Hazard for several days. Since my position was actually split between four stations, I was technically under the direction of WYMT in Hazard for the first several years of my employment. This was despite the fact that I was trained at WKYT, lived geographically closer to the Lexington station and my paycheck was printed at distributed by WKYT. I know it seems confusing but later everything would be handled by WKYT from a management point of view.

After more training and guidance at WYMT I spent the next several days driving around my coverage area introducing myself to various contacts. My office was located at The Center in Somerset and consisted of a TV bureau news set and office. I had the ability to sit at a news desk and go LIVE or record "look lives" from the set and then I could feed up my stories via a unit called the telestream which is basically a VCR looking box that uses high speed internet or T1 lines to feed up stories. A 2 minute news story basically takes about 10 minutes to feed to either WKYT or WYMT. Sometimes WBKO or WVLT in Knoxville would take my stories depending on where the story originated.

Although over the years I have covered news all over central Kentucky, my position is generally focused on southern Kentucky including Pulaski, Laurel, Whitley, Lincoln, Adair, Russell, Wayne and McCreary counties. Some have told me they think I cover news in one of the most interesting geographic areas not just in Kentucky, but in the United States!

So after nearly a month of training I was ready to embark into the world of television news. I honestly think that everything I had learned in college, radio, and journalism had prepared me for what was about to happen. And what you're about to read is a sample of the some of the most unique, sometimes outrageous, and even bizarre stories I've been a part of the past 10 years. As I've often said after many of these events, you can't make this stuff up!

# CHAPTER 12
## THE FIRST STORY

I'll never forget my first assignment. But it's basically a story of how a story was given to me and then taken away. It was early December 2003, and I remember arriving at the Somerset office about nine that morning and scanning the local newspaper for story ideas. I remember seeing an article about a man arrested on voyeurism charges for videotaping school children at several school playgrounds. I called the WKYT newsroom and pitched the story idea to them. The producer thought it was a great story, but she then said something that took a lot of the wind out of my sails about doing my first "real" story for the news.

"Well, I think we're going to send down another reporter to 'help you out '" she said.

What ended up happening was that the Lexington newsroom didn't have a lot of confidence in my abilities just yet and they wanted their crew to do most of the work. Basically, if I crashed and burned….*they wouldn't get burned.* So what happened was..I interviewed the local police spokesperson about the story while another crew from WKYT did almost the exact same thing. It was like two crews from the same station competing against one another. At the time, I was a bit insulted but what happened in the end was me doing the story exclusively for the WYMT station and the other crew doing it for WKYT. So I didn't have to do as much work, only having to edit one story instead of two. And to be honest, the other crew *was* more skilled and experienced and they were able to get more content for a better story. Plus, when I got back to put my story together I discovered that some of my interviews were out of focus, thus the quality wasn't all that it should be.

A few days later I would do my first package for WKYT. It was a simple story about a new road called the Monticello improvement project. A new 4-lane highway would replace a narrow, dangerous tunnel under a busy section of railroad tracks. I thought it was a good story because it highlighted the need for the new road with interviews from the mayor and drivers mixed with concerns from a business owner that a new road would draw traffic and commerce from his store. As it turns out, the business owner's fears became reality because not long after the new road opened, he went out of business.

I would do stories on a unique rabbit farm, tourism, and a few odds and ends. It seems like at first WYMT had more confidence in my abilities but it didn't take long for me to win over the top brass at WKYT and for them to realize I was capable of the "big story."

My first "big" story would come on Christmas Eve, of all days. And what made it cool was that it would be the first story seen by just about everyone on my dad's side of the family, the same people that I told to watch what I thought was to be my first story the day before Thanksgiving that never happened.

Holidays are usually slow news days and days before holidays like Christmas Eve are no different. Most people take them off, government offices are closed and you're left depending on "breaking" events to cover. And that's what happened on that day.

The day started like most days. Usually the first thing I do is pick up my cell phone and make my beat calls, calls to police, 911 centers and the like to see if anything happened overnight. My call to the Lincoln 911 center turned up gold.

Firefighters had just left a home north of Stanford where a mobile home had been destroyed by fire. It seemed at first like a typical home fire story, but the fact that it was on Christmas Eve made it a little more interesting. "A family… loses everything in a house fire….on Christmas Eve." It was the kind of story that would create sympathy..but there I was about to learn more that made it even a bigger story. And that was the "hero" element.

We found out that a 12-year-old boy was being called a hero for helping his siblings escape the burning home in the middle of the night. His mother, grandmother and siblings were being treated for injuries at the local hospital and the medical staff allowed me and other reporters to interview them. What's more, when word got out that the family had lost everything, including their Christmas presents in the blaze, the doctors and nurses went out shopping and "our cameras were rolling" as clothes and toys were delivered to them. It was great stuff.

So I took all of this footage and went to the bureau in Somerset and put it together. Then I picked up the phone and called my dad and told them that they would be able to see me that night. My dad lives outside Louisville but I knew that night they would be with other relatives in Paris which gets WKYT. So my dad, mom, brother, grandparents, aunts, uncles, and cousins would all see the first big story from me. I couldn't be prouder in what I thought was a job well done.

And now for the "rest of the story." Several months later, an arson indictment was returned from the fire. As it turns out, the 12-year-old's grandmother wanted holiday sympathy and intentionally set fire to her home so that people would give her and her family stuff for Christmas. Bizarre. Again, stuff so weird..you can't make this up!

The new year in 2004 would bring more big stories and soon I came to understand why my position and, more importantly, the area I cover would be so crucial to WKYT.

# CHAPTER 13
## THE "LIVE" SHOT

One thing that makes local TV news so important is the 'live' shot. When you see the reporter standing outside a "scene" talking about what just happened or what's going on. I had worked for two months and still had not done a live shot where a LIVE or SAT truck would be sent to me to feed back. In the ten years I've been with WKYT, live reporting has changed drastically but when I started the only way to feed pack live stories was with a satellite or microwave truck. A satellite truck was necessary in the area I cover because the distance is too great for a microwave signal to reach the station in Lexington.

I thought my first live shot would come with a story in London on Jan. 15, 2004. I was sent to London, Kentucky because a man had just been arrested for allegedly bringing a bomb into the London police department. Here's the quote from the police spokesman I interviewed:

"He said he didn't have any weapons with him, but he said 'I do have a bomb.'"

Now keep in mind that at this time we are only a few year removed from the September 11, 2001 terrorist attacks and any talk of a bomb would cause anyone concern. The subject in this story did in fact have a device taped to his chest. The ATF, state police and others were called and they discovered the device would not have detonated but the subject was still charged. I remember the mug shot of the guy was freaky. His eyes were all bugged out and he had this look that was part fright, part confusion.

WKYT immediately knew this was a big story so they rolled the SAT truck, what they call "BIG SAT" to me. I was to be the noon top story, which the producers called, "off the top." So I got to London, had the interviews and b-roll shot and at 11:15 that morning no SAT truck. As it turns out the SAT truck would not be coming because another story was developing on the interstate. And that turned out to be an even bigger story than the one I was working on.

The reason the SAT truck was held up was because three men were stopped for having a mobile meth lab in their car. The fumes coming out of the car were so strong and toxic police shut down the interstate and made the subjects strip naked in front of everyone to be decontaminated. And our news crew was right there to get it all, well all that we could legally show on TV that is.

So I did a noon "phoner" instead which is basically just a phone report talking about the bomb guy. The packaged story with video and sound would air later on the 5 p.m. or 6 p.m.newscast.

So I missed out on my first LIVE shot but that would come later. And that story would be even bigger.

## TRAGEDY

I've heard it said many times by others in my profession that news crews have a difficult job in the fact that we are meeting people in the worst times of their lives. Police, EMS, first responders, firefighters, etc. are there in accidents, murders, fires and other events that could also be labeled tragedies. And we're there also…to tell the story of what happened.

Before getting into TV news I was like many who complained about TV news people always going up to families after their loved ones were killed and asking the "tell me how you feel" question with the microphone stuck out and camera rolling. Geez, have a heart, buddy, they've just lost someone, how to do you think they feel? But since I've become one of "those people" I've come to understand this whole situation and have learned a much better and more professional way of handling it.

I was called to McCreary County on a cold February day in 2004. The story was a carload of people killed, hit by a train as a grandmother was rushing to take her grandkids to school. What a sad story, but it was also very newsworthy. Again, the SAT truck was rolled to me and this time a mobile meth lab didn't stop it from getting to me. The SAT truck got to me just a few minutes before my first LIVE shot so I only had a few minutes to gather my thoughts and was quickly thrown in front of the camera. And it was a straight live shot, meaning all I did was stand in front of the camera and talk for a minute or so about the accident without any video rolling. I was a nervous wreck and I think I talked a mile a minute and probably rambled on for too long, but it was my first time in front of a LIVE camera so I think I did OK.

The story was so big it warranted what we called a side-bar. I was reporting on the nuts and bolts of the train vs. car accident but another reporter was called down to focus more on the victims, who they were, what they'll be remembered for, etc.

But as the story was developing, lots of family of the victims responded as well. And needless to say, I and other reporters were there asking family members for interviews. I've since come to understand more of the process in asking relatives for interviews immediately after a tragedy. It's not that I want to interfere with their grieving but I've come to understand that a lot of people *want* to tell their loved ones' stories and the news media provides them an avenue to do just that. But I've always been the type of reporter and person that I'm not going to beg for an interview.

The story would turn out to be one of the bigger stories of the year and warranted follow ups. That's when something happens that later results in another story. The railroad crossing was one of many in the area without lights or cross bars and people in the area claim it had resulted in other accidents. One person interviewed said a man being rushed to the hospital having a heart attack never made it and died in the car because a train held him up. The people in that area didn't just want lights and cross bars. They wanted a bridge over the tracks. I and other reporters did several follow ups and I believe the issue even made it into some legislation dealing with railroad crossings and safety.

# CHAPTER 14
## ICHTHUS

One of the things I absolutely love about my job is being able to cover stories that I watched others cover that seemed to *enjoy* covering. One of these is the annual Ichthus Christian Music Festival in Wilmore, Ky.

Ichthus is the Christian version of Woodstock and in fact it started in the early 1970s as a Christian response to the secular event. Every year since then thousands of people, mostly young people, flock to a field in Wilmore near the Asbury Theological Seminary for several days of Christian rock music concerts. I've attended Ichthus almost every year since I was twelve.

Ichthus wasn't always an event that the TV news media covered but for some reason, it became an annual story in the mid 1990s. Crews would usually show up in a LIVE truck and have several reports during the weekend, and usually the story had some kind of weather angle. That's because Ichthus was held for years in April and often there was either a lot of rain, thunderstorms, tornadoes, mud or all of the above. In fact the last year the event was held in April, it even snowed!

Reporters given the Ichthus assignment seemed to have a lot of fun both putting the stories together and reporting live from the event. Usually the packages were full of mud covered kids, shots of hippie looking youngsters with nearly every hair style imaginable, and video of groups blasting out rock and roll music with lyrics focused on Jesus.

I've always loved Christian rock so covering Ichthus seemed like the best of many worlds. I would get to take in some wonderful music yet I would be working at the same time. Yet during the last weekend in April 2004, I think I got a lot more than I bargained for!

2004 was the 35th event but it almost didn't happen. Like I said, Ichthus was all about music and ministry but some would also say it was known just as much for the mud. And in 2004, Ichthus became "Icky thus." And I was there right in the middle of it.

Ichthus started on a Thursday that year and that's also when the rain started. It rained all day Thursday and by the time the first campers arrived, they barely got in the campground when their vehicles got stuck. You can imagine what happens when you get thousands of vehicles trying to get into a huge grass field from a two-lane road after hours of rain. You get a mess. And it was a huge mess.

By Friday morning festival organizers contemplated cancelling the festival because so many couldn't get into the festival grounds and those already there didn't know if they were going to get out. So a compromise was found. Those already there for the festival (since they really couldn't go anywhere until the grounds dried out) were allowed to stay but no one else was allowed in. I was already en route to the festival to cover it when I found out that a news conference was called. It was there when all of the changes were announced and plans were laid out for continuing the festival.

Later that day, when the music finally started, I covered my first Ichthus festival. I admit, I had tears in my eyes and I got quite emotional standing there with my gear shooting video of bands such as Sanctus Real, Petra, and Audio Adrenaline playing. Here I was covering an even that for years I was just a spectator for.

And part of what made covering Ichthus '04 so much fun was being able to interview the youth minister that took me to my first Ichthus in 1982, Mark Walz. Mark was such a big influence on my life as a teenager and seeing him at Ichthus was a real joy. Mark was there with both his kids and the youth group from the church he was the minister at in eastern Kentucky. Mark loved God and he loved bringing kids to Christian events that aim to strengthen their faith. In fact, I think Mark was one of the few people that could say in 2004 that he had attended all 35 Ichthus events. It didn't bother him that mud was everywhere, the skies were cloudy, and more rain was on the forecast.

My news director wanted me to focus on a specific youth group and how they were dealing with the weather so I focused on Mark and his kids. And it was one "sound bite" that he gave in talking about the weather that was so simple yet so profound to describe just how muddy the festival grounds were.

"This is the lava flow of mud," he said.

He was exactly right! The mud so widespread that it flowed like lava.

As it turns out, the skies cleared up and after Friday I don't think it rained again. It was a great weekend and I think I turned out some fabulous packages that highlighted the message, music, and of course how the mud took center stage!

Later I was also able to use the footage I had shot during the festival to produce a two part series on the growing popularity of Christian music. One of the lines I used in my story was that according to CCM Magazine, there were twice as many Christian rock CDs sold in 2004 than in 2003. Some of the people I interviewed for the story at Ichthus said they enjoyed Christian rock because it sounded more like "real music," it reminded them of "why they are here," and it wasn't offensive.

In December 2012, Ichthus organizers ended their long run of annual festivals but it was actually predicted the end would come about a year and a half before then.

The problem was that the festival had lost money every year since the dates for the festival switched from spring to summer because of widespread weather problems. Having a summer event as opposed to a spring event meant they started competing with mission trips, vacations, and other festivals.

"We used to get 3,000 from Michigan. Now we get 300 from Michigan," Ichthus President Mark Vermilion said.

The festival once attracted 20,000 but it dwindled to just 14,000 in several years time. Festival organizers hoped to sell the property to a buyer who then would lease it back to them just for the dates of the event. It never happened and the 2012 event would be the last summer event at the Jessamine county location.

# CHAPTER 15
## EMOTIONAL ISSUES

In the news business, you cover lots of stories that deal with a lot of emotions. And opinions. The wet/dry issue is one of these. Kentucky is a unique state in that not every town or county allows alcohol sales. There are 'wet' areas and there seems to be even more 'dry' areas. And whenever there is a wet-dry vote, you see those communities divided in half. It seems on one side you have people claiming alcohol sales are needed for economic growth and on the other you have people claiming booze will be the detriment of society based on religious or moral reasons.

My first wet-dry election occurred in the town of Burnside, a small town bordered Lake Cumberland. Burnside, pop. 627, hadn't had a drop of legal liquor sold in 70 years, but in May 2004 voters approved the alcohol referendum by a mere 50 votes. It not only became the first city in the region to go 'wet' but it became the first Lake Cumberland town to adopt legal liquor. Burnside seemed to set the trend for other wet-dry elections and within a few years alcohol would flow in nearby Corbin, London and eventually, Somerset.

Burnside was a unique example because the town of only 600 or so people swells to thousands on a few weekends during the summer because of the tourists and boaters that flock to the lake. Those who wanted to legalize liquor sales argued that a few restaurants selling alcohol would only make the area more attractive to more tourists.

The arguments against alcohol were from those who said beer and wine sales would increase DUI's and crime.

## RATS!

One of the biggest stories I did in 2004 dealt with rats. Some even cringe today when I talk about this story. The thought of big, hairy, disease infested rats will make some shriek and some shuddered when watching my coverage of this issue.

An old milling company in Somerset was infested with rats and some neighbors were worried about the pests getting into their property. I was told these rats came out at night so one night I went to the milling company, set up my camera, turned on my camera light and sure enough I got coverage of dozens if not hundreds of rats running all over the place. Some were quite large. Some neighbors said they saw rats as big as cats. I'm not sure I got coverage of animals that big but the rats I saw were much bigger than your household mouse.

The neighbors we interviewed were worried about local officials not taking them seriously so they called the news media. We interviewed them and then went to the city council when a few concerned citizens took their complaints to the local government. A few days later the health department set up rat bait and before long the rat problem was no more. Some claimed that the local officials took the issue a bit more seriously once the news media got involved.

## "24"

One of my favorite TV shows is "24." It's about a federal agent who always saves the day I the nick of time. I think I find it attractive is because number one the main character always does the right thing regardless of how it hurts him or others close to him and because there are many parallels with how we are always getting our news assignments done in the nick of time.

In the TV show, each season is one 24-hour day with each episode focusing on one hour of that day. And in May 2004, I had a day that seemed like a marathon with so much happening I felt like the main character of the show.

It was May 26th and severe weather was in the forecast. The day started out like any other. I think the main story assignment was a preview of the tourists expected on Memorial Day weekend. But when that story was done I was told to go Lincoln County for storm damage. As it turns out a tornado had damaged several homes in Kings Mountain and one structure affected was my wife's grandmother's barn! So I ended up interviewing my mother-in-law for the story that night. I ended up working a double shift and by 11 p.m. I was home thinking my day was over. Yet it was just beginning.

I went to bed about midnight only to be woken up at 1:30 a.m. by a phone call from the overnight producer telling me that a tornado had just destroyed a trailer park in Somerset. I reminded the producer that I had already worked a double shift but they asked me if there was any way I could go out and cover the event so I said "yes." I arrived about an hour later just north of Somerset to find numerous trailers destroyed yet miraculously few people hurt by a tornado. I did numerous phone reports and later did a LIVE shot for the noon shows then recorded some 'LOOK LIVES' for the 5 and 6pm news. By 3pm it was time to go home. So I had basically worked from 9:30 to 11 p.m. then from 1:30 a.m. to 3 p.m. A month later the marathon shift earned me a 27 NEWSFIRST PRIDE

FIRST award which is more or less like an employee of the month award.

## The Unsolved Case or Mystery

If there is one kind of story I've covered more than anything else it's the mystery or unsolved case. A missing person who hasn't been found. A murder without an arrest. And there seems to be lots of these in the area of southern Kentucky I cover. One of the first such stories I covered was about a mother and son found dead in Pulaski County.

Linda Gibson and her son, Cody Lee Garrett were found in a field just outside Somerset in July of 1994. In July of 2004 I did the 10-year anniversary story of this mystery. Police said they had several suspects but nothing to make any arrests. Later I would cover mysteries surrounding the disappearances or deaths of Charles Randolph, Kevin Price, and Kara Rigdon. All happened within a thirty to forty mile area but there's nothing to show that any of them are related.

## "ROADIE"

People love stories about children and it seems they respond even more to stories about animals. And a story in July 2004 about a dog named "Roadie" resonated with thousands of viewers!

On July 19th, 2004, our first story about Roadie hit the air. It was about a beagle mix that was tied to a bumper of a car and then dragged. Police told us the car probably got up to 25 miles-per- hour. The dog survived but she was severely injured. So much that one of her back legs was amputated and she lost a lot of fur from the road burns.

Somerset Police say after the dog's owner realized what he did, he got out, untied the dog from the bumper, tied her to a pole and fled. I don't believe police ever made an arrest or had any persons of interest of who the owner or suspect was. But the heartwarming part of the story came in how the community responded with donations and offers to care for the dog after learning of what happened through my stories and others in the media.

I remember when Steve Crabtree interviewed me for the job he told me that I would find my greatest joys in being a reporter in the stories that prompted others to do good. And "Roadie" stories were just that. Within days of our first stories airing, people called the vet with offers to adopt the dog and to inquire about donating money for her care. In one story I said that "Roadie has captured the heart of the community."

The clinic Roadie was treated also served as its adoption agency and before long it was flooded with offers to adopt the dog. One lady dropped by the vet with $100, touched by Roadie's story her gift was in memory of a dog she had recently lost to cancer.

I remember going back and doing several follow up stories and one conversation with my then news director, Jim Ogle that comes to mind.

"Now, Phil, this is the type of story that keeps people talking. I want you to call that vet every day from now until they adopt that dog out. We CAN'T miss out on that part of the story, you understand?!!!" he said.

I think Jim was afraid that if we took our eyes off the story even for a day we stood the chance of getting beat on it. WKYT was and still is in a tight ratings battle with the NBC affiliate in Lexington and any big story we cover we want to stay on top of to get the information *first* so that we can in-turn broadcast that first. The ironic thing is, I think WKYT was the only TV station to cover the Roadie story but regardless, whenever there was an update, big or small, I was doing a package on it. Eventually Roadie was adopted by a center in Lexington that provides assistance to the elderly and she became somewhat of a mascot to the residents there. Roadie would become one of the first high profile animal stories and one I would cover later focused on a dog in Pulaski County led to a new felony type of law dealing with animal abuse.

# CHAPTER 16
## WASHINGTON, D.C.

I think I've been fortunate in that my job at WKYT has literally taken me a lot of places. And that may seem odd for a one man band because most trips require a crew of several people. But in early 2005, a southern Kentucky case became a national story in the nation's most important courtroom.

In October 2004, the U.S. Supreme Court agreed to hear the case concerning public displays of the 10 Commandments. Steve Crabtree once told me that no other issue draws more attention and controversy than those dealing with faith and religion. And the 10 commandments issue was a biggie.

It all started when a judge-executive put up a display of the 10 Commandments in the McCreary County Courthouse. The American Civil Liberties Union got involved after a local citizen complained. All the while the courthouse in Pulaski County had a similar display. Long story short, the arguments for and against the posting of the 10 Commandments worked its way to the nation's highest court. The case in southern Kentucky asked simply if the posting of the religious text was fitting and proper alongside other historical documents such as the Magna Carta and Declaration of Independence.

The Justices would hear two cases. One being if the 10 Commandments could be put back up beside the historical documents in Pulaski and McCreary Counties and the second one deal with a stone monument of the commandments on the lawn in front of the state courthouse in Austin, Texas.

The sides were clearly drawn. County officials in Pulaski and McCreary Counties were joined by numerous church groups in supporting the commandments but those from the ACLU who believe that the separation of church and state means keeping God, the 10 Commandments and any other religious lingo from state government or taxpayer funded facilities.

My boss, Jim Ogle, agreed to send our chief photographer, Kenny Harvener and me to Washington, DC to cover the U.S. Supreme Court considering the cases in February of 2005. Despite Kenny or "Harv" as he's referred to in the newsroom, going, it actually started out as more of a one man band assignment. Harv and I met in London early on a cold, snowy and slippery morning in London. We drove together to a church in Corbin were commandments supporters would be boarding a bus for a trip to DC. I was going to ride the bus with supporters and get interviews while Harv followed in the WKYT SUV. We decided that I would spent about an hour on the bus getting interviews and video of people riding the bus, then when the bus stopped in Middlesboro I would get out then we would feed a "look live" back for noon.

For some reason, and I don't remember why, I wanted to get out of the bus earlier than Middlesboro. This decision almost ruined the entire trip! I was talking with Harv via cell phone and we decided that when the bus stopped at a railroad crossing, I would get out and hop in the WKYT car and we would proceed onto the WYMT news bureau in Middlesboro to feed up the noon look live.

The problem was it had been snowing and while most of the road was clear of snow and ice, the emergency lane was still ice and snow covered. And because the bus only stopped for a moment to let me get out, when I saw Harv in the WKYT car a few car lengths down, I took off running toward him. BIG MISTAKE! Not two or three feet from the bus, I slipped. It was definitely one of those "feet flying out from under you" moments. I came down hard on my rear end and the camera hit hard on the battery end. I wasn't hurt but I was more concerned about my camera.

"Are you alright?" Harv asked me as I was getting into the passenger side of the Ford Escape.

"Yeah, only my pride is hurt!"I said, laughing.

But a closer look at the camera revealed a nightmare. There was a big, long crack in the back casing and I knew the camera was toast and would never make the trip to D.C.

The good news was we were just a few miles from the WYMT 57 Mountain News bureau and there was an extra camera there. So we drove to a UPS facility, shipped the broken camera back to WKYT and we picked up the replacement camera. A near tragedy for sure, but it all worked out in the end.

The broken camera combined with the weather delayed our arrival in Washington. We had hoped to get there early enough that night to a preview story from the Fox News building, but we were too late so WKYT ended up airing a pre-recorded piece from Lexington.

We checked into our hotel, got a few hours of shut-eye and early the next morning jumped into the Ford Escape for our drive into DC.

Keep in mind that before this day, all of the stories I had ever covered, whether in radio, newspaper, or television were stories that would mostly be of interest to central or southern Kentucky views but this story, in the nation's capital was of interest to a national and perhaps even a world-wide audience.

The story was on CNN, Fox News, MSNBC and countless other news channels. And I was there, too,

After checking into the Fox News building with my editing equipment, Harv and I parked the Escape in a garage below and caught a taxi to the Supreme Court. By the time we got there thee were already demonstrations both for and against the posting of the 10 commandments. We interviewed supporters from Kentucky who made the trip, got them marching around the building and praying and balanced it with a few ACLU supporters. I recorded an "in" and an "out" and Harv caught a cab back to Fox News to feed back my story for the noon news. I got with the rest of the media waiting in line to watch the arguments before the justices.

We just a few years removed from 9/11 and security was extremely tight getting into the nation's high court. I remember waiting in line, going through a metal detector and then having to wait in a trailer outside the courthouse before being called to wait in another line before we were allowed in the main chamber. I think our day began at 5 a.m. but the arguments didn't start until almost noon.

Cameras and recording devices aren't allowed in the Supreme Court so the only thing I was allowed to do was take notes in a notepad. I sat several rows back from the Justices surrounded by large marble columns and the artists whose work would make it onto TV sat right in front of me. They must have spent hours on the craft, working from the outside-in on the drawing, starting the columns first, saving the Justices and attorneys for last with renderings of them pointing, attentively listening or just sitting. It was quite impressive, being there, knowing that I was sitting in the same room where countless arguments of national importance were decided.

The arguments lasted several hours and when done, I went back outside were a large podium of it seems hundreds of microphones were set up for attorneys to give an impromptu news conference. We rolled on that, got a few more interviews, and drove back to Fox News where I would put together stories for the 5 and 6 p.m. news that night.

Putting together the stories wasn't easy because of all the legal lingo addressed in the arguments. I can't remember a lot of what was said, but I do remember the Justices seemed to side with those who wanted to commandments kept in courthouses. After logging what seemed pages of sound bites, I wrote my stories and then walked up several flights of stairs to the roof of the building. It was there where I would go LIVE.

The background for my shot was impressive. You could see the U.S. Capitol dome over my left shoulder, all lit up in the night sky. It was incredibly cold that night but just standing there, in one of the most important cities *in the world,* was an incredible feeling. I was thinking, "just a few years ago I was a news director for one of the smallest radio stations in Kentucky and now I'm standing in Washington, D.C. for a story with national significance!"

Plus the story had to do with faith. Now I'm not going to get into whether I think the 10 commandments should be in government buildings, but I must tell you, any time a issue that has to do with God becomes part of my job, that is very important to me.

After several live reports for WKYT, WYMT WBKO and WVLT, it was time to drive back to the hotel. And it was late. We recorded a look live for the 11pm and by the time the day was over, I think I had a story in every newscast. But it was worth it. Harv and I stopped at a Red Lobster for a late dinner and then crashed in our hotel room. The next day we drove back into DC for an interview with U.S. Rep. Hal Rogers on homeland security, then we drove back to Kentucky.

Later than year in June, in a tight 5-4 decision the Supreme Court ruled that the commandments were in fact unconstitutional and had to come down.

# CHAPTER 17

## The year of "the trip"

2005 was a year that I felt as if I lived out of a suitcase more than my chest of drawers at home! The day after Harv and I got back from D.C., my wife and I loaded up the kids and we spent a few days in Pigeon Forge. Then two days later Harv and I joined a crew in Atlanta for coverage of the SEC Men's Basketball Tournament.

Covering the SEC tournament was another opportunity to cover an event that looked like it was fun to cover. And it was. Don't get me wrong, it was a lot of work. But something happened that week near the Georgia Dome that made that year's tournament one of the most memorable news events for even the veteran photographers and reporters who covered dozens of events.

The SEC men's basketball tournament is a huge event for Kentucky. The men's basketball team has a long history and tradition of doing well in the SEC and many in Kentucky schedule vacations around the tournament. It's usually 3 or 4 days of basketball games in either Atlanta, Nashville, or New Orleans. For a reporter, your assignment is to find fans and cover whatever they're doing. Whether it be watching games, going out to eat, buying fan gear or simply hanging out. And during the Friday morning of that year's tournament, tailgating turned to terror. In fact I even used that line in my stand up story!

I was roomed with our assignment editor/field producer and that morning we were getting ready. We had the TV on some national news show and there was word of a man who shot and killed a judge in an Atlanta courtroom and then ran out into the streets.

"Gee, I wonder if that guy will come anywhere near the tournament," my producer half-joked.

I say "half-joked" because that gunman did come near the tournament! In fact he was so close that later that day SWAT teams walked among tailgaters and others getting ready for the tournament.

One second you're getting ready to throw down a hot dog and the next you're looking at a cop in camouflage gear carrying a long rifle! This went on for awhile but eventually the gunman was captured a few blocks away. Still, all the excitement made for an interesting angle to the tournament stories. Harv would later tell me that that SEC tournament was the most exciting one he ever covered because of the courthouse shooter story.

Over the next several weeks I would drive to Missouri for my grandmother's funeral and then unpacked and packed again for a trip to Austin, Texas for the second round of the NCAA basketball tournament.

I wasn't supposed to go on the Austin trip but was called on after another photographer backed out in the last minute. So my job was to drive a LIVE truck to Austin and then do fan packages, camera work and whatever else for the coverage of the Kentucky Wildcats in the Regional final of the 2005 NCAA Men's basketball tournament.

The SAT truck driver and me arrived in Austin several days before the tournament was to begin. The first assignments were to do some introductory stories of what Austin had to offer so that fans coming from Kentucky would know what to expect about the community. We did a story about how bats were prevalent in the city and one on the popularity of the Austin City Limits music program that aired on PBS.

We had heard that there were parts of Austin where people simply waited at dusk for all these bats to come out. And sure enough, near downtown by a river, tons of people were just sitting out waiting to see bats! So Ben, the SAT truck driver, who was also a photojournalist went down there and interviewed people waiting to see bats and then got video of the thousands of them flying out.

There's one thing about Kentucky basketball. Their fans will travel to see them during the post season, no matter how far it is. We got them coming off the tour buses, as they were going into the hotels, at the pep rallies and then going in and coming out of the arena when the games were played. Kentucky won their first game against Utah but barely lost their second against Michigan State. The loss was bittersweet for several reasons.

Before leaving home I was told that if Kentucky won both games and advanced to that year's Final Four, not only would I be required to cover the Regional Final games, but I would be required to drive the LIVE truck to St. Louis for the Finals. That would basically mean more than two weeks from home. My daughter, who was 5 at the time, knew her Daddy was going to be gone "as long as Kentucky was winning." So she prayed that Kentucky would lose so I could come home. Some would say that was very sweet, but I know others would like that was sacrilegious in a state like Kentucky!

Anyway, I guess you could say Hannah's prayers were answered because Kentucky did in fact lose and soon I was on my way home. That would be the last trip for awhile and the last basketball tournament trip until was called to be on the crew for the 2011 Final Four trip.

# CHAPTER 18
## SAD, SAD NEWS

Whether you're a muti-media journalist or a traditional reporter, all of us have to cover really sad stories from time to time. It doesn't get any sadder or more difficult when the job requires you to approach family members of children killed in accidents. One deadly crash in May of 2005 in particular comes to mind.

A 5-year-old was riding in minivan just after her mother had picked her sister up at the local fitness club. The van ran off the road, hit a pole, and rolled over. Sadly, the 5 year old was ejected because, while she was sitting in a booster seat, her seat belt wasn't fastened. The little girl died and obviously her parents were devastated.

Here's a challenging situation. It's an obvious news story that needs to be covered. A little girl not properly fastened in a car seat is killed. I was able to interview police and the family minister so there wasn't a need to approach the family for reaction. I was satisfied with the "sound" I had. But I do remember running into another TV news crew and the day after the crash, they were going to "ambush" the family at the funeral home just to try to get an interview with them.

I'm not about to tell other reporters how to do their job but there are some things *I'm* just not going to do. If I am desperate to get a family's reaction to a tragedy such as things, I'm not going to go after them at the funeral home where they are trying to gather enough strength to make the most difficult arrangements of their lives. I may call the funeral home and have them ask the funeral if there's anything they would like to say, but in no way am I going to just show up and go after them.

As it turns out the little girl's family *did* want to do an interview. Several days after the crash, the girl's mother and father agreed to a sit-down interview talking about what a wonderful daughter they had just lost and the tragic consequences of not buckling her in properly.

The mother told me that she didn't buckle the little girl in because she was in a hurry and it was raining. Ironically, the rain caused the van to hydroplane and ultimately, crash. But the main message the family wanted to get out was how they wanted to thank their community for all the support they had received in the wake of their incredible loss.

This story aired before Facebook, Twitter or most social media caught on like wildfire. So most of the support the family had received was because they had heard about the story on the news or from reading it in the newspaper. So in turn, they turned to the news to thank everyone for the help they had received because of what others had seen on the news.

## SERIOUSLY?

We cover serious news but often you get to cover stories that you have a hard time keeping a straight face reporting. Such was the case on May 10, 2005 when I covered a man arrested for getting a DUI……on a horse. Yes, don't mean to beat a dead….horse…but again, you can't make this up.

What made the story so fun and interesting was it was one where all the pieces came together very easily. When you're running both the camera and the reporting duties sometimes you don't have as much time...and in this business, time is everything.

I went to the police station and got the official police spokesman interview about the facts of the case. Police say a state trooper was off duty when the horse "jumped" out in front of him. The horse was then pulled over and the man was taken to jail because as police told us, "you don't have to be driving a car to face the offense of drunk driving."

Later that day, I drove out to where the alleged drunk horseman lived and sure enough, he wanted to "give his side of the story."

He admitted in our interview to drinking about a half case of beer and jumping on his horse for a 10-mile-ride into town. The man admitted he was intoxicated but he didn't think he was endangering anyone else so he thought he should just be charged with alcohol intoxication and not driving under the influence Police argued and said a horse can be defined as a vehicle under state law. The funny thing is, he was arrested again for almost the exact same offense just a few months later.

## The High Profile Court Case

You've probably heard a television news anchor introduce a story and describe it as a "high profile" case. Usually it's about a murder or a shocking killing or something about a death that makes it unique, unusual or just downright tragic.

In late June 2005 my first high profile case started. A young man had just picked up a some friends late one night in Somerset and was driving them down a road that ironically was called "Bourbon Road." A sheriff's deputy turned behind the car to follow it. The Mustang sped off, lost control, left the road, crashed into a wide utility pole, severing it. The accident killed a young woman named Brittany Shoap. The driver, Ryan West, was charged with murder. Several other young people were in the car but they escaped serious injury.

Brittany was a local beauty contestant and had won numerous pageants. Her mother was very outspoken during all the court proceedings and demanded justice for her deceased daughter. She said she was proud of her daughter in the fact that she was wearing her seat belt yet the accident was so violent she was killed anyway.

The Ryan West case was of the few cases that every time he was in court, whether it was just a simple proceeding or a major event, we were there too. And so were all the other local TV news stations as well as the local newspaper and radio stations. And after every proceeding, Brittany Shoap's mother was available to talk to the media in giving her reaction to what had just happened.

The court case took months and a trial wasn't scheduled for nearly a year after the crash. During every pre-trial hearing, I was usually the only one man band. But during the trial, I was going to receive some help. WKYT send down a photographer to handle the camera duties so I could just focus on reporting the events. I remember thinking there was no way to cover a trial as a one man band, but since then, I believe I have covered every trial as a one man band.

But the trial of Commonwealth Vs. Ryan West never happened because he ended up pleading guilty to a lesser charge and was eventually sentenced to 10 years in prison.

# CHAPTER 19

## Hurricane Katrina

As I said before, 2005 was the year of "the trip." From the 10 Commandments case in March to the SEC and NCAA tournaments to regular vacation trips, it seemed like as soon as one trip was over, it was about time to go on another one. One of the most memorable trips came unexpectantly after that year's worst natural disaster.

Hurricane Katrina was the most devastating hurricane to hit the US mainland in decades. The category 5 storm with winds of 175 MPH and killed more than 1,800 people. It caused billions of dollars in damages and almost destroyed the city of New Orleans. Thousands left that community and never returned. It was a huge national news story and because of the widespread devastation, many Kentuckians donated their time and money to help the gulf coast recover.

About a week after the hurricane, a decision was made by the WKYT news director, main anchor Sam Dick and our chief videographer, Kenny Harvener to send a crew to cover the Kentuckians that were trying to make a difference. At first just Sam Dick and Kenny Harvener were going to go but then I was asked to go along as well to cover some additional "one man band" stories.

I remember getting the call to go on the trip while I was sitting outside my house having a yard sale on Labor Day weekend.

"Phil, this is Jim (Ogle), we're sending Sam Dick and Kenny to the gulf coast to follow the Salvation Army and others helping the folks in New Orleans and I'd like you to go along, too.," Jim said.

"Wow," I said. "Let me think about and I'll call you back." Now honestly my mind was already made up but because of the "dangers" associated with the trip, I had to talk with my wife about it. Later my wife's grandmother learned of the plans and worried that I was going make my wife "a widow" because she had heard about the violence in New Orleans after the storm, especially around the Super Dome when some people attacked and shot at relief workers. However, our trip was nowhere near there; we stayed exclusively in Mississippi around the Biloxi area.

After talking with my wife, I made the decision to go. Sam, Kenny and I would meet in Frankfort on Labor Day Monday and follow in our vehicles a crew from the Salvation Army. Kenny would shoot for Sam and I would go out and get my own stories. I was a crazy week. And there were a lot of uncertainties even before we left.

The hurricane destroyed or weakened many gulf oil and gasoline operations and gasoline became in short supply. Never before had I experienced pulling up to a gas station when the clerk said you could only buy a few gallons. But that happened at almost every station south of Tennessee. So we didn't know if we would even get to the gulf coast. And once there, where would we stay? Almost every hotel was destroyed or full of people whose homes had been wiped out or severely damaged. We packed camping gear knowing we could very easily be spending the week sleeping in tents. I also packed by power inverter knowing we would probably have to charge our gear batteries and power our editing equipment from the car battery.

We left Monday from near Frankfort and after a pit stop in Bowling Green we were headed south for Biloxi. We followed the crews from the Kentucky Salvation Army Kettle trucks, which are actually called "canteens." They fix meals and drive around, delivering them to whoever is in need.

We finally arrived in Biloxi on a Tuesday night. My first story was focused on the Salvation Army volunteers and why they were doing that they were doing. Our first night was spent at an old shrimp packing company in a tent. The next day Sam and Kenny did a more in- depth story on the Salvation Army canteen crews. I went up north for a profile piece on Kentucky State Police helping a town that despite being miles away from the coast, still dealt with widespread damage from the hurricane force winds. The second night we spent on the coast in a hotel that had lost power but was still being used by news media and others willing to brave it. I don't think I've every slept in a room hotter than that room was. And we had to manually pour water into toilets for them to flush.

The entire week we worked out of the CBS News path Satellite truck, which stayed parked on the beach for both the national correspondents and local affiliates that wanted to feed back stories. There were news crews from as far away as Nevada covering the aftermath of the storm.

The third day of our 'adventure' had me covering a Kentucky family that now lived in Biloxi and the arrival of a semi truck filled with everything from bottled water to mattresses that had arrived from Lexington to a Catholic church which would then set up a center to pass out the donations.

The Kentucky family lived a good ways inland yet they still suffered significant damage to their roof. But they had electricity. Their children were with their grandparents in Kentucky so we each had our own rooms! What a nice change from what we experienced the days before. So each night we were in Biloxi we stayed in a different place. One night a tent at a shrimping factory, the next at a dark, hot hotel and the last in a nice cool home in a bedroom decorated with Sponge Bob Square Pants and Disney characters. Oh the places this job has taken me!

We ended up staying just one more day and the last day my story focused on a church in southern Kentucky helping a town in southern Mississippi. A Somerset church had found a town, called "Wiggens" that had not received much aid or support from other relief groups and the Somerset church basically arrived "just in time" with food, water and other supplies to help them.

My story had interviews with town folk that basically said had it not been for the giving people in southern Kentucky, the people in the southern Mississippi town would not have had what they needed in the days after the disaster.

I ended up submitting my stories for the annual Associated Press Broadcasting awards and once first place in my division for my stories of Kentuckians helping the hurricane victims. But the real honor was being a part of history, in covering good-natured Kentuckians giving of their time, money and efforts to help others.

A few months later another assignment would take me back to the gulf coast, this time as sole as a "one man band." A group from Eastern Kentucky had collected $10,000 in toys for children in one Biloxi elementary school. The school was flooded in the hurricane and most of the children were living in temporary trailers or shelters since their homes were destroyed or heavily damaged. No room for a tree much less any other holiday cheer. The school was located one mile from the beach and four feet of water filled the school after the hurricane.

Celebrating the holiday was considered a luxury that year for many families but a few people in Kentucky wanted to make sure every child in that school had Christmas presents. So on the last day of school before Christmas break, while all the kids were in the cafeteria watching The Polar Express, a handful of volunteers delivered Christmas presents to every classroom. When the movie was over and the kids thought they were going back to their classrooms to gather their things for the long holiday break, they went back to their rooms to find their desks filled with presents. Tons of toys, even bikes, were waiting on them. And my camera was there to capture it all. What a story. It was hard holding the camera and keeping my eyes dry!

"Well there's no greater feeling that giving," one volunteer told me. "But I hope these children learn that when they grow up and they see something that is devastating, something that happened to them, I hope they open their hearts and give to others."

## Same 'Ole, same 'ole

One of the more interesting things about being the "Southern Kentucky Bureau Chief" is where this job has literally taken me. I cover a large area: Pulaski, Laurel, Whitley, Wayne, McCreary, Russell, Adair, and then even sometimes in Lincoln, Rockcastle, Casey, Boyle, or Mercer Counties. And more often than not, it seems I end up in the same places over and over again.

One of these places is "Canada town" in Whitley County. Canada town isn't an incorporated city, it's a community in northwestern Whitley County that's probably home to several hundred or maybe thousand people. It's like many places in southeastern Kentucky where 'everyone knows everybody' and like the name implies, many "Canada's" take up residence there.

I'm not going to get into why certain places are "hotbeds" for news, I'll let you figure out that one on your own. But Canada town always seems to be a location for news and it seems controversial news which resulted in a phone call into our newsroom where our news director usually had to deal with an unhappy viewer over something we said or reported on.

My first trip to Canada town was on August 18, 2005 for a deadly fire. A 19 year old mother, her three-year-old son, and the mother's 23-year-old boyfriend were killed. The initial investigation did not pinpoint a cause but the *suspicion* was that it was started by a pot of beans left on the stove. Family members disagreed and that's what led to the phone calls to our newsroom. They were upset that we reported three of their loved ones basically died because of a cooking accident.

Later, I'll get into other stories from this unique part of Kentucky. Like the couple allegedly beat up by their grandson. Or the young lady from there brutally murdered by her husband who then was accused of holding several people hostage in a Somerset trucking company. Or the interview with the father whose son was one of two suspected of starting a fight that a teacher and state lawmaker was seriously injured (and later died) trying to break up. And there was the story that resulted in another call to our newsroom because of someone who gave me permission to shoot video on property, that supposedly she wasn't authorized to give permission for!

Every day I get up and usually don't know what story I'll be working on. That is what makes what I do more of an adventure, than a profession. It's like a box of chocolates, borrowing from the line in the movie, *Forrest Gump.* You never know what you're going to get.

News is always taking place. You can never predict when something is going to happen and sometimes you have extremely slow news days when it seems you can't buy a story. And then there are days it seems everything blows up at once. And occasionally as soon as you're done reporting on one story, another breaks. And your day just got very long.

October 12, 2005 was one of these days. I had just finished working on that day's assignment when I received a call from one of my "sources" in Wayne County. When I worked in radio news in Stanford about the only way I could find out about stories was listening to the police scanner, receiving a news release or getting a rare phone call from a listener or an official with information of something breaking. Listeners rarely called with news and sources were a dime by the dozen. But in TV news it's been a lot different.

Recently I was looking over my iphone and counting all the contacts I have. There are more than 300. It's a varied bunch of officials, police officers, "regular Joes" and the like that I depend on for tips and information. And sometimes these people will call or text me with tips that can result in big stories. WKYT's chief photographer, Kenny Harvener told me about people like this during one of the long conversations during my training in November 2005.

"You'll need a long list of contacts to call every day asking what's going on," he said.

"Sounds like I'll be busy," I replied.

"Yeah, but after awhile instead of you calling them for news, they'll call you," he said.

I admit that I didn't believe it because of my experience in radio news. People never seemed to call but I must admit that Kenny was absolutely right. I admit now I don't have to call people usually when something big happens they either call the station or they call me direct. I have police officers, coroner, EMT's and other officials who will tip me off on stories. And if it wasn't for them, we either wouldn't get the story or we would get beat on it. And if you're reading this right now and you're one of these people, please know that I appreciate you helping me do my job more than you'll ever know.

One of these people, whom I'm not going to identify, lives in Wayne County. He wouldn't want to be identified or to receive the credit for what he does. He calls or texts me all the time with tips of what is going on because of where he works and who he knows. Usually his tips are gold and they result in significant stories. On October 12, 2005 his tip turned into a big story…albeit one that was a tragedy. But had he not called, we probably would not have known about this event and we possibly would have been skipped by the competition.

Gary Catron was a teenager who lived on Missouri Hollow Road. On that fateful day in October he took off on his bike like he probably did every day but on that same road was a man that police said was under the influence of alcohol. The car struck Catron's bike and he was killed.

The man behind the wheel was charged with murder, DUI and leaving the scene of an accident because they say they ran from them after hitting the boy. Police said Roger Smith was drunk. Smith's criminal background showed several alcohol intoxication charges dating back to the late 1990s.

This story became a high profile event that resulted in the news media in the courtroom just about every time the suspect was. And the victim's family was there as well. Very little happened with his case though because our records at WKYT show that he was ruled incompetent to stand trial and was later admitted to institutional care.

# CHAPTER 20
## Oakwood

If I had a dollar for every story I did about a place in Somerset that most know as "Oakwood" I may not have to every work again. I say that as a joke but stories about Oakwood dominated the local news and newspapers in Somerset for months from late 2005 into 2006 and several times after that.

Oakwood has gone by several different names. The Communities at Oakwood, Oakwood Community Center, and now it's known by Bluegrass Oakwood. Whatever it's called its purpose is simply to provide a residence type setting for mentally challenged adults. But in the mid 2000s the facility was the subject of numerous investigations, indictments, citations and stories of caretakers charged with crimes.

My records show that the first story I did about Oakwood was on October 26, 2005, but I'm sure there were previous stories that aired on WKYT before my time. The story was rather simple. A man was accused of hitting a mentally challenged resident at Oakwood. We interviewed the suspect's wife who said that her husband was simply trying to defend himself and others against a resident who had become violent.

The investigation against that suspect and the many others that followed eventually made its way to the Kentucky Attorney General's office. And today when there are new investigations it's usually handled at the state level. Recently I was trying to track down news on a recent arrest and every call to local authorities, whether Somerset Police or the Pulaski County

Sheriff's office was came back empty but once I got a hold of the state, everything was confirmed.

The problem that eventually made its way to even the United States Department of Justice was that Kentucky's Inspector General was trying to prove a pattern of abuse by numerous workers at Oakwood. My story on October 26th contained this line that would pave the way for what was about to happen: "The attorney general representative here today stated that this case is just one of several alleged cases of patient abuse at Oakwood. She says that it's very possible there could be other indictments similar to this one before this investigation is over."

That's what I said in my "stand-up out," that last thing you see and hear the reporter saying, usually standing outside in front of the facility or subject of the story.

Problems at Oakwood even threatened the facility's attempts to stay open because a big part of his lifeblood was in the form of federal funding. And in November of 2005 I ran a story on how Ky. health officials were appealing a decision to cut off Medicaid funding because of the numerous citations and arrests at the facility. That funding accounted for more than half the Somerset facility's budget.

On November 7, I reported how 8 citations were leveled against Oakwood, which at the time was Kentucky's largest institution for mentally challenged adults. There were 300 residents and more than 1,000 employees. A new management team was brought in, hoping to correct some of the problems there. It wasn't just a few bad employees beating up residents there that was the problem, according to what investigators were saying. It reached all the way up to how those employees were *supervised.* Basically, if the boss of the organization is behind the problems, you've got a very serious problem.

The stories of alleged abuse were outrageous. One resident cut himself with a compact disc. Another ingested paint. One was reportedly thrown into a wall. Others were allegedly beaten by the people who were supposed to be caring for them. And in a few severe cases, the residents even died. Investigators said they wanted to find out how far knowledge of the abuse went.

One day I and reporters from the two other Lexington stations were joined by local print and radio media in "camping" outside the grand jury room of the Pulaski County courthouse. Inside jurors were going over hundreds if not thousands of documents. In fact the "money shot" that day was getting video of attorneys literally rolling in the boxes of documents on a dolly. During that story I reported that investigators were looking at abuse that dated back 4 years. That meant some of the alleged beatings by caretakers started in 2001! But for whatever reason did not come to light until late 2005.

I remember one of the reporters asking a question to the attorney general representative as to why someone who cared for vulnerable adults would resort to beating them. His answer was classic:

"I've not ready any job description that says you have to serve the resident, provide meals to the resident, bathe the resident....and to beat the resident."

My lead-in voice track to that sound bite was:

"Most of the evidence presented to jurors deals with people working directly with patients. That can be a tough job, but investigators say abuse is no excuse."

I was there in Feb. 2006 as Governor Ernie Fletcher toured the Oakwood campus and promised changes. Ironically, the facility would receive its 15th Class "A" citation of alleged abuse from something that happened the day Fletcher was there.

"A resident who was known to be aggressive kicked another resident so badly that it caused life threatening injuries," was said in my Feb. 15, 2006 story. The incident happened about 7 that night, hours after the governor left. The citation or reprimand dealt not with the attack or the kick, but rather because "staff did not document the majority of instances of the client's behavior and that interventions were ineffective in controlling his behavior," according to the report.

In August 2006 I reported that Oakwood had received more than 20 Class "A" citations. Some workers actually rallied that year stating problems in being overworked was causing stress that ultimately led to workers engaging in behavior that resulted in resident injuries or problems.

I can't remember what happened with every case but in August 2006 I reported that one of the first people charged with abuse pleaded guilty to an amended charge of reckless abuse of an adult by a caretaker. The judge ordered him to serve 60 days in jail and to accept a lifetime ban in patient or resident care.

"He's agreed to never look for that type of job again, never to work in that type of job again and that's an extremely important result," Mary Cartwright with the Kentucky Attorney General's office told me in the story that aired on August 19th of that year.

But not everyone charged was found guilty. Two of the more high profile caretakers were exonerated. They were charged in the drowning death of a mentally challenged resident in 2005.

"It's hard to justify why some group from Frankfort in the attorney general's office would come down and get involved and get an indictment in a case that had been fully investigated,"

Jerry Cox, one defendant's attorney told me on Jan. 25, 2007. Cox was adamant that the state should not have investigated what he thought should have been left up to local authorities. In fact, in 5 cases handled by the Kentucky Attorney General, none resulted in guilty jury verdicts, according to what WKYT reported in early 2007. No one from the AG's office commented on my story.

We would report further cases of grand jury indictments and arrests in the months to come but ultimately Oakwood did not lose out on their funding and was able to stay open. There's been a few more arrests over the years but nothing like the dozens of indictments reported on in the mid 2000s. Oakwood's management would eventually be taken over by a Lexington organization called "Bluegrass" and since then, Oakwood has more or less stayed out of the news.

# CHAPTER 21

## Road to change.

In the 10 years I've been in the southern Kentucky bureau, I've seen a lot of changes come to Pulaski County. Most of that has come in the form of new roads. Now you can argue if some of them were needed or not, but the bottom line is for the most part, it's easier and in some cases, safer to get to and around Somerset.

The first story I covered for WKYT dealt with the Monticello Street project. The new 4- lane railroad overpass replaced a tiny tunnel that semi trucks used to get stuck in. And it made getting from areas south of Somerset into downtown much easier.

In late 2005 construction started on a new section of 4-lane U.S. 27 north of Somerset. It was a section of roadway I would travel frequently to get to the bureau at The Center for Rural Development. The new 4-lane section of 27 replaced the two lane busy roadway from Eubank to Somerset.

I would see and do stories about the new 4 lane bridge spanning Lake Cumberland on Ky. 90 in Burnside, the 4-laning of Ky. 1247 from the 914 By-pass to 27, and construction of the northern bypass which could one day become Interstate 66 in southern Kentucky. All in all, state and federal money has paid for millions of dollars in new and improved road projects, much in the form of 4 lane highways to replace dangerous and heavily traveled pathways that had been the scene of accidents.

I remember interviewing business folks who said the new roads would also attract more commerce to the area. Others said it would lead to inconveniences as one part of the new U.S. 27 actually caused an electronics store and food mart to close.

# CHAPTER 22

## Wolf Creek Dam and Lake Cumberland

On November 30, 2005, the anchors at WKYT read a small story that would become a much larger story weeks later. It would become a story that started out as a local story only the Somerset newspaper covered but would become a very high profile event that affected thousands of people and caused some to fear for their lives and even lose their livelihoods.

On that day in November the VOSOT simply stated that "workers at wolf creek dam say they're confident a seepage problem will not cause a major problem for Lake Cumberland.. or those who live downstream." The story that lasted about 30 seconds went on to say that water was seeping below the dam that holds back the massive southern Kentucky lake. The leaking water was not visible but a $300 million repair job was still scheduled to fix the problem in 2006. The last line of the voiced over copy leading into the "SOT" or sound-bite said all this was done to "prevent dam failure."

It seemed rather simple and straight-forward, yet that last line changed the story all together. If Wolf Creek Dam was to fail, Lake Cumberland will become Cumberland River and everything downstream all the way to Nashville would be flooded. Lake Cumberland was a major source of recreation but it created livelihood and jobs for thousands. And it contained *a lot* of water. So much that it could cover the entire state of Kentucky with more than 3 inches of water!

That simple vosot would become the first of numerous stories in what began as an "advisory" of what sounded like a routine repair job but would turn into a major repair job that drastically changed the way the lake looked and how people would use it. And eventually jobs would be lost, businesses would close, and lives would be forever changed.

One of the more memorable stories I did leading up to the story announcing the multi-million dollar repair job focused on a man named Willis McClure. In the story that aired in late November 2005, I started out with NAT (natural sound) of him playing his organ.

"Visit Willis McClure and chances are he will sing you a song or play one of his historic organs," is how the story started.

McClure lived just below Wolf Creek Dam and I interviewed him because if the dam were to fail, his would be one of the first houses to be washed away by the tidal wave wall of water. In the story he told of how he used to ride a boat to Jamestown High School on the old Cumberland River, before the dam was built and Lake Cumberland was formed. He talked about the big flood of 1937, how he watched his father build the dam, and how in 1970 he helped fix the first leak at the dam that threatened his family's property. When I interviewed him, he was actually employed by the U.S. Army Corps of Engineers as a janitor, so the dam had always had a big impact on his life.

Yet the leak didn't bother him.

"I'm not afraid at all," he said in the story."'Cause I don't think it would break fast enough to get me out of there."

Yet others were afraid and some media even played on those fears. One reporter from a station not in central Kentucky told me that his assignment was specifically to "go and find people scared to death the dam will fail and they will be washed away."

Later I find out that some people were so afraid that they even slept in life jackets.

In late 2005 the U.S. Army Corps of Engineers said the repair job would take 7 years and cost hundreds of millions of dollars. Such a massive job that Congress would have to approve it.

"Yes, we'll find the money," U.S. Rep. Harold "Hal" Rogers told me in the Nov. 29, 2005 story. "It has to be done. We can't let the dam continue to seep water an risk possible danger later on," he said.

It would basically involved pouring a concrete wall into the mile long earthen portion of the dam.

Long before the work started, water was taken out of Lake Cumberland to relieve pressure off the dam, exposing parts of the basin not seen in years. Old U.S. Highway 27 and building foundations were visible in parts of Burnside. Docks that would normally float were on dry ground. Ducks were walking where the previous summer they were swimming. But perhaps the most devastating sight for many was the many boat ramps that ended in dirt…instead of water. Businesses that depended on boats going into the lake knew they would soon see their profit literally dry up.

"In the last 10 years I have not seen the water this low," a boater told me in a story that aired on December 1, 2005.

In early 2007, we found out the repair job was more serious than first thought. That's because the U.S. Government discovered that Wolf Creek Dam was in high risk of failure, so that the lake would need to be lowered by 10 more feet.

And my story took me to the Alligator marina in Russell County. I interviewed a man who had recently purchased the marina. He was concerned, and rightly so, because the boat ramps would soon not reach water and much of his dock would soon be in extremely shallow water.

"680 feet (the lake level elevation above sea level), is not going to allow us to do services that we did in the past, we won't able to pump gas," he told me in the Jan. 22, 2007 interview. He was one of the many impacted when lake-lowering translated to about 40 feet of water taken from the lake. Ed Slusher was one of many who questioned if the government was telling people the "whole story."

"They don't want a panic situation. I don't think they really know," he told us.

Eventually he made the decision to move the marina to a deeper location.

"We're losing 60 to 70% of our revenue for the whole season," he told us during an April 2008 story. Thus he decided to move the entire marina to deeper water. At the original site, the marina was in zero to 3 feet of water. The new location, at Cave Springs, would put the docks in 90 feet of water.

I didn't get to cover the actual move but the marina owner took pictures and I used them in the story. He called it a 7 hour labor of love to move the floating city 6 miles down the lake.

He spent a lot of money to move the dock but his move did not pay off and eventually his marina was sold in an auction. His was a tale common to others, but perhaps his was the most severe. He didn't just lose his business, he lost his livelihood and my camera was there to follow every step of his sad story. From the cold winter day in 2007 when he feared the worst…. to the auction of his business in April 2011.

That man's marina was probably the largest problem but dozens of other docks soon found themselves on dry land or close to dry land.

"We lost our electric, we lost our water, we lost our club and now we're having to start over," a member of the Somerset Boat Club told me on Jan. 24,2007. The Somerset Boat Club on Pittman Creek in Lake Cumberland was around as long as the lake itself. Yet the lowering of the lake ended its long run in the narrow channel of water. More than 80 boat owners find themselves working feverishly on cold winter days to move their houseboats in the icy water.

"It could cost us a million dollars or more to get back to where we were," the boat club president told us.

Others spent a lot of money also. The owner of Lee's Ford Marina, JD Hamilton told me that he spent more than $2 million moving his docks from low to high water and then back again. And he also lost when some boaters stayed away.

"General business dropped that first year about 30%," Hamilton told me.

Hamilton told me that he felt that the U.S. Army Corps of Engineers should have done more to help marinas, which through no fault of their own, suffered through the lake lowering.

"Right now I pay them $230,000. They are demanding rent while the lake is under an emergency,"

Hamilton wanted the Army Corps to forgive rent payments while the dam work was underway or to at least ease up on lease restrictions.

It can be said perception is reality. The perception that the tourism industry dealt with over the next few summers was that Lake Cumberland wasn't just lower, parts of it were bone dry. Some other media came down and only showed parts of the lake with coves filled with mud instead of water. So the perception was that no one would be able to get their boats in or that there wasn't enough water to do much of anything.

As a result, parts of Lake Cumberland normally busy in the summer were virtual ghost towns. Boaters who usually flocked to Somerset, Jamestown or Wayne County went to Laurel Lake or lakes in northern Tennessee instead. Or they simply stayed home.

On January 26th I traveled to Frankfort, Ky. to work out of the bureau in the state capital covering a meeting of local, state, and federal officials in determining a course of action for the dam.

"We have a tremendous amount of instrumentation within the dam and all of the instruments say the dam is not in imminent failure," an official with the U.S. Army Corps of Engineers told a room full of reporters that day.

Officials did tell us then that Kentucky's 3rd largest lake… and 9th largest in the nation…could have been lowered further, yet it never happened. In fact the project was actually finished sooner than expected. In 2012 Levels were gradually brought back up in the spring of 2013. Yet for some, the damage was already done.

"Six of 11 marinas were either in bankruptcy or out of business," Hamilton told me in April 2013.

He was one of many marina operators who had to move his docks to higher water and then back again once the water levels were raised. Lee's Ford had 800 slips so he said it was like moving a small city. The good news was that the fix at Wolf Creek Dam was labeled as a "100 year" fix so that no one expects to see this kind of situation ever again in their lifetimes.

# CHAPTER 23

## Kentuckians help West Virginia Mining families

On Jan. 2, 2006, one of the nation's worst mine disasters occurred in Sago, West Virginia. A blast trapped 13 miners and only one survived. The disaster was the focus of the world's attention and media descended upon the tiny town for weeks. And in Kentucky, a small group in the once bustling mining community of McCreary County wanted to help.

A telethon sponsored by a local cable TV station and home oxygen company raised thousands for the mining families. I covered the telethon and the trip to Sago to hand deliver $2,000 checks for each of the 12 families impacted by the loss.

"We're not asking people to give from their wallets, we're asking people to give from their hearts," one of the telethon organizers told me in the Jan. 13, 2006 story.

Time and time again in my career that's been the sentiment I've been given a front row seat to, and the story I've been able to share with thousands of viewers. There's no greater feeling that doing good for others, and no greater joy in the communication industry than sharing that message with others.

Early one January morning I met the group in Whitley City and drove hundreds of miles with them as they made the quick trip to Sago. Once there I covered the checks being hand delivered to the minister of the church that helped the mining families. Despite the fact that the tragedy had happened weeks before, the town still had a bad taste in their mouth because of all the national media that had descended upon their town for days. I wasn't allowed in the church with my camera.

"You see that right there?" a church member said, pointing to a part of the church foyer.

"Uh, yeah," I said, not knowing what he was talking about.

" That's where I threw (a member of the national news media) out," he said.

Apparently one of the national correspondents didn't obey when told to leave the church and was literally thrown out, and the guy was letting me know that he would do the same to me if I didn't do everything he asked. Obviously the people were devastated by their loss and felt that some of the national media had only added to their problems.

I admit that sometimes we do get in the way, but other times we can help people by getting word out of their tragedy that in turn results in others helping. It's a fine line and the key is being part of the solution, not the problem.

# CHAPTER 24
## Missing

It has to be one of the worst things a family could ever go through, second only to dealing with a death. Not knowing where a loved one is, or what happened. A Russell County family is still dealing with this mystery that began in January of 2006. And unfortunately it's a tale I've had to tell too many times in southern Kentucky.

Christopher Gregory was last seen on January 31 of that year.

"I mean nobody knows nothing. Russell County is a small town. Somebody should know something or saw something. I mean it's like nobody knows anything," his mother Rhonda told me on March 28$^{th}$ of that year.

The only thing police did find was his driver's license, but searches turned up no significant leads. We interviewed Rhonda Gregory numerous times over the next few months and even years later but to this date what happened to her son remains a mystery.

Over the next few years I would do missing person stories about Charles Randolph in Casey County, Kara Rigdon in Marion County, Adam Hogan in Taylor County and Jeffrey "Kevin" Price in Pulaski County. Hogan and Price's bodies were found but their cases are either unsolved or contain many unanswered questions as to what happened and/or why.

I have contacts in my phone of relatives of each of these families. Usually on the anniversary of their disappearance or death, I will call them and do another story. Sadly, it's almost like you could just rewind the tape and play back the same story you did the previous year because those families have the same questions they did then.

## Family violence

Perhaps nothing can be worse than a member of your own family charged in a crime that involved hurting you. Earlier I told you about Canadatown and the numerous stories centered on the quaint community. On June 29, 2006, I interviewed the couple attacked by their grandson, who was charged with their attempted murder.

"Right now all I can do is pray and tell him to trust in the Lord because the Lord is the only thing that can help him now," Wayne Gilbert told me about his grandson, Tyler Politte.

Gilbert and his wife, Helen were some of the nicest, friendliest most God fearing people that I have ever met. And they told me that it was talk about God that somehow set their grandson off and triggered a violent side of him.

"And he started slashing me and he broke a handle out of one knife, and he went and got another and broke that handle," Gilbert said of the terrifying ordeal.

Gilbert crawled away to get a gun while his grandson went after his wife. He heard the horrifying words directed at his wife from his grandson's mouth.

"Granny, I've got to kill you, too. Can't let you go on. " Gilbert said he heard his grandson say.

Tyler Politte and another man were caught and arrested. Both were charged with attempted murder. Despite the horrifying ordeal, the couple still had a positive outlook.

I think that's what is so satisfying about meeting people like the Gilberts. Despite everything they went through, not just being attacked in their home, but at the hands of their beloved grandson, they still kept their faith strong and ended the interview and our story with an encouraging word and promise of good that could still come from it.

Recently I was speaking to a group of middle school students during a career fair. One of the students asked me how I could cover so much bad news and how hard it must be to always be reporting on tragedies. It's true, it's not easy, but I also told that student that sometimes tragedies present opportunities for everyday, ordinary people to do good.

For example, let's say a young person is killed in an automobile accident. The tragedy not only devastates the family but leaves them with unexpected medical and funeral costs. How are they going to pay for it? I can't tell you how many times we've covered that story but at the end we've put a bank or location that people can donate money to, and because of our story the families had enough money donated to pay those costs. That's a great example of good coming in bad and how the media can help, and not hurt!

# CHAPTER 25
## Flight 5191

In August 2006 I had a part in covering one of the biggest stories not just that year, but one of the biggest tragedies to ever affect central Kentucky. And not just central Kentucky, but many areas all over Kentucky and the nation.

Comair Flight 5191 crashed shortly after take-off on the morning of August 27, 2006. Only one person, the co-pilot, James Polehinke survived. I was actually one of the few reporters who was not called into work the Sunday of the crash. That was actually one of the rare times one one man band was not called in, because most of the crews working that day were made of reporter and photographers working in live trucks. In the days and weeks that followed, I covered numerous follow-up stories that focused on several of the victims.

All of them had stories to tell but perhaps the saddest was about the newlyweds killed en route to their honeymoon. And they were from Laurel County, an area I frequently cover news in.

John Hooker and Scarlett Parsley Hooker were married in what many described as a storybook wedding on Saturday, August 26th, 2006.

"He was just all happy, smiling. Talking to a lot of people. You would just see him staring and smiling. Saying is this real?" a friend of the couple interviewed for the story the Monday after the crash told us.

My story focused on Hooker-Parsley wedding and we aired their wedding video as part of it. In fact when the story aired on WYMT-TV I was told the female anchor couldn't read the anchor tag because she got so choked up. It was a true tragedy and obviously touched on a lot of emotions.

John Hooker was a well-known baseball player who had played for both North Laurel High School and UK, and his bride, Scarlett was a cheerleader. Both were very well known in both Laurel County and Lexington and their story made national news.

"Saturday night it was the beautiful beginning. Sunday morning brought the tragic end," was how I described the couple in my narrative.

In December 2010, Texas Rangers pitcher Brandon Webb asked to change his number to 33 in honor of his former teammate at UK.

"For Brandon to be able to wear that, it's just going to continue to make us see that as we watch him, because of his number," John's brother, Adam told me. John Hooker and Webb both pitched together at the University of Kentucky and were close friends afterward.

There were several other southern Kentucky and south-central Kentucky connections on Flight 5191, including the owner of a well-known skating rink and a Danville man who was on his way to Atlanta to start a new career in pharmaceutical sales.

Then Lincoln County coroner Bill Demrow's sister and her husband Clark and Bobbi Benton were killed. The husband and wife were on the flight to celebrate Bobbi's 50$^{th}$ birthday. Ironically, Demrow was one of several coroners called to the scene to identify victims and he found out en-route to Lexington that his sister and brother-in-law were among the victims.

"I just made my peace with it," Demrow told me in the August 30$^{th}$ story. "Decided that I needed to continue on. Do what I was trained to do. Plus, that would get me there, and I would get information that I needed. That my family needed," Demrow said.

Demrow was no stranger to tragedy, both locally and on a nationwide level. He had seen the worst of the worst in local accidents and crimes but he was also called to the Gulf Coast to identify victims of Hurricane Katrina the year before. I'll never forget seeing him get choked up during the interview, and here was a man that had seen death closer and more intensely than you and I will ever see it.

"It's very tough. That would be my two youngest sisters. There were six of us children. Now it makes two that we've lost," he said, holding back tears. Demrow was talking about another sister who had died tragically a year and half before.

I don't remember how many of the funerals we covered of Flight 5191 victims but the Benton's graveside service was very memorable. The couple left behind two children, who released doves into the sky at the cemetery.

"They have left this earth, and they've done so together. That's just representative of the life they had with each other," the officiating minister told me after the service.

## UPLIFTING

Earlier I talked about covering the good in times of bad. And in October 2006 I had the opportunity to sit down with a true survivor who nearly died in 2004.

In October of that year James Rains, 70, was missing in the Daniel Boone National Forest near Laurel Lake in Whitley County for almost a week. We covered how search and rescue crews were trying to find him but I was able to track him down for an exclusive follow- up two years later. The reason I pursued the story then was because another man went missing in that same area and we wanted to show that it was possible to survive in the woods "without food, shelter and not much water" for days.

Rains had quite a story and that was an understatement. He told me on Oct. 26, 2006 that he went five days without seeing another human being or eating a bite of food.

"You're so cold…You couldn't get warm. I didn't have matches to build a fire," Rains told me.

Rains credits God in helping him survive.

"And the biggest problem I had since I'm a Christian was the devil, aggravating me all the time," he said.

Ironically, Rains was found by fishermen fishing in a place where boating is not allowed. When the nurse came up the mountain to check on him she couldn't find a pulse.

"It was so weak. My heart was beating so slow," he said.

But he made it out and told me that if it wasn't for his bad leg, he would have joined in the hunt for the other missing man.

# CHAPTER 26
## Frankfort, Ky.

In late 2006, my job title changed from Southern Kentucky Bureau Chief to part-time state government reporter. That's because the powers that be at WKYT wanted a one man band to cover the Kentucky General Assembly in early 2007 and I was the only one man band they had.

So in January of 2007 I would leave my home at 8 and make the one-hour drive to Frankfort to cover the legislature. It was an interesting assignment completely different from the usual general assignment stories I would cover in southern Kentucky. I would usually start my day covering a committee meeting involving some kind of high profile, emotional issue then end the day covering lawmakers bickering over the bill in either the House or Senate.

I was part of the "press corps" working in the Kentucky state capital. I had an office just below the Kentucky Senate chambers and would occasionally sit in front of a "set" with a state capital backdrop and report the goings on from Frankfort. Other times, though, I would set my camera outside the office with a view of the inside of the rotunda in the background. On days when school groups visited the capital, I admit I receive a lot of stares and some strange looks when I was juggling my camera, a light set and extension cords, trying to get just the right amount of illumination on my stand-up shots! It was also a prime example of getting the "monkey in the cage" look from people as they walked up, looking at you as if you're some kind of zoo animal on exhibit.

Covering state government was exciting, yet challenging. I have covered everything from casino gambling, animals rights activists seeking tougher pet protections and families demanding safer coal mining laws.

One of the most emotional issues I covered in 2007 was when several women whose husbands had died in coal mining accidents pleaded with lawmakers for safer mining conditions. I'll never forget the shot I got in a committee meeting, of one woman weeping, while holding a picture of her little girl kissing a picture of her father who died in the mines the year before. Her cries were answered because that year the Kentucky legislature did in fact pass tougher laws and some would argue that coal mining is safer now because of those bills that I witnessed become law.

## Miss USA, then misery.

In the summer of 2006 most of the nation, and probably every TV set in Russell County was tuned to the Miss USA patient as a girl from small town Kentucky won the biggest pageant in the nation…Tara Conner won Miss USA.

I interviewed the new Miss USA in Somerset and spoke to her parents of the incredible victory and "girl from small town USA" making it big.

"I've had to overcome some obstacles because I am from a southern state," Conner told me on June 9, 2006. "People hold certain opinions of southern states , which is great for me because I get to prove how wonderful our state is."

But several months later another national story concerning the winner came out. Several New York newspapers had reported Conner tested positive for drugs and was photographed partying wildly.

"A nightmare. Of course we were hoping none of it was true," a resident of Russell Springs told me amid allegations that the Miss USA was 'partying, drinking, and engaging in questionable behavior.'

I was in Russell Springs to gauge reaction when Donald Trump made the announcement via a news conference that WKYT carried live that Conner would be allowed to keep her crown despite the allegations.

"We're sure she is going to turn this around and make it even bigger thing than before. She will be a better Miss USA than she would have been to begin with," another resident told me.

"She…everybody makes mistakes as a teen. Hopefully she will learn from it. I think she will do better," another friend of Conner's told me.

# CHAPTER 27

## Lincoln unsolved murders…then answers.

Some of what's in this book could probably make stand alone books. The murders of Ryan Shangraw and Bo Upton in February 2002 is such a case. The 18-year-old Upton and 20-year-old Shangraw were shot and killed in Shangraw's trailer on that cold winter day and for years, no arrests were made and no suspects named. It was truly a mystery that would not be solved for 6 years.

I didn't have any role in covering the story until much later. When the crime happened, I was working in at WVLK radio and we simply aired updates from the crime covered by one of the other Lexington TV stations. But every year on the anniversary of the murders, WKYT interviewed the victims' families and my first year covering this story happened in 2007.

"Your mission in life doesn't need to be searching for murderers," Bo Upton's mother, Sherry Moore, told me in February 2007. No one had been arrested despite a $25,000 reward, web sites formed dedicated to the unsolved case, letters to congress asking for more funds for police in similar cases and dozens of prayer chains formed. In 2008 those prayers would be answered.

"The guys who did this they're watching this tonight, I guarantee. One day I'll look them in the eyes, I hope I can hold back," Moore said in the story that aired the year before the first arrest.

That first arrest came in April 2008 when police say a suspect finally turned himself in. As it turns out that suspect was already in jail in Madison County serving a 2 year sentence on unrelated offenses and was charged based on DNA evidence that matched him to the crime scene. Police suddenly had the evidence when Campbell spat out a bag of cocaine he was trying to smuggle into the jail. The DNA on that bag was a match to DNA police found on a bandana recovered at the crime scene.

"I'm glad we have a DNA database. Because without Jamarkos Campbell's DNA on file, these guys would have gotten away with murder," Commonwealth's Attorney Eddy Montgomery said after a court proceeding.

"I just prayed with faith that it would be solved," Bo Upton's mother told me on July 25th, 2008. "But I didn't know when. But this year, I had a feeling it would be soon,"

Police ended up charging four others. Testimony was that three, one of them a juvenile at the time, traveled from Richmond to Stanford on Feb. 1, 2002, and fired multiple rounds into Shangraw's trailer, but five were all responsible in one way or another. One defense attorney said one was simply the driver and that the death penalty should be excluded for him. Another who reportedly never fired a shot was the mastermind behind the entire thing, despite testimony being that he simply waited in the car while the murders took place.

"As a general rule, if three people go and rob a bank, the driver is just as guilty as the three people who went in, as a legal matter, I see no difference in those kinds of things," Montgomery said after the court appearance.

Evidence that came out during the legal process was that Jamarkos Campbell, Deonte Simmons, and Matthew Tolson were inside the trailer when the shootings happened while Neccolus Mundy and Charles Smith waited outside in the car.

Testimony came out that the shootings were allegedly gang related and attorneys talked of the teardrop tattoo on Campbell's face. Prosecutors told me that in some gangs a teardrop tattoo meant "you killed someone." His attorney wanted that kept out of the trial.

"When I saw them, I was thinking how could you murder a human. Their poor souls must be evil people to just murder people and walk off," Moore told me after one of the court appearances. There were two girls, friends of the two boys in the trailer at the time and police said they could have easily been killed as well, and it was probably a miracle it wasn't a quadruple murder.

The shootings happened not long after a homecoming basketball game at Lincoln County High School, Moore said that her son, Bo, had left the school to go see Ryan and he was basically in the wrong place at the wrong time when the 4 burst into the trailer, guns blazing.

"What was going through my mind, is that 'God, I have prayed for this for 7 years,'" Moore told me after a January 3, 2009 court appearance.

The first defendant to face trial was Jarmarkos Campbell. It was originally scheduled for April 2009 but was pushed back two months because of issues with ballistic evidence.

In May the long awaited high profile trial finally started. The day before, I interviewed Ryan Shangraw's father, who still lives just down the road from where his son met his violent end.

"I want to know what happened that night," Shangraw told me from his kitchen table. Not a lot about the motive from the crime came out during the pre-trial hearings but police had said robbery was one reason for the crime. Shangraw also said drugs were a factor.

"I know what kids do. And adults for that matter. Smoking pot, different stuff. I knew he did that, but I didn't know anything about drugs. They talk like he had all kinds of money," Mr. Shangraw said.

Campbell was the first arrested and his apprehension resulted in a domino effect of the other four suspects named. Police testified in the trial that Campbell and the others traveled from Richmond to Stanford to steal cocaine, but they left empty-handed. Prosecutors said Shangraw was a dealer. Tolson testified against Campbell

"Go get the cocaine, to rob them," he said on the witness stand.

But both Upton and Shangraw were shot and killed instead. Shangraw was killed first and witnesses said Upton was killed as he was trying to hand over his wallet. More than 24 rounds were fired and bullet holes riddled the tiny trailer.

Tolson said from the stand that they only wanted to steal Shangraw's cocaine supply but "something went terribly wrong." Gunfire started and it ended with the two young men dead. Two girls were hurt in the hail of gunfire and testified during the trial.

"Bo stood up. Grabbed his wallet. And he tried to give it to them. Kind of threw it at them. And then the gentlemen, the men got scared and they just shot Bo. He fell toward the TV. They kept shooting. They ran out the door," one of the girls said.

The 24-year-old Campbell was convicted of wanton and intentional murder. He was sentenced to 25 years without the possibility of parole on June 30$^{th}$, 2009. Jail was not a strange place to the man who was 16 when Upton and Shangraw were killed, as evidence came out that he had been in and out of incarceration several times on drug offenses.

"I'm sorry that two mothers have lost their boys. But I'm really sorry that I've lost mine, too," said Campbell's mother after the sentencing.

Eventually the other suspects would admit to their roles in the shootings and no one else would face a jury trial. On July 13th, 2009, Deonte Simmons, Neccolus Mundy, and Charles E. Smith pleaded guilty, ending months of denying they had anything to do with the crime.

"I think what it took was Jamarkos Campbell going to trial. The jury recommended the maximum consecutive (sentence). That was their motivation," the prosecutor said after the men entered their pleas.

It also came out during the court proceedings that Simmons may have been the only one who fired the fatal shots, yet five people went to prison for the murders.

"In my opinion all five of them..all five are guilty," Upton's mother Sherry Moore said after hearing the please. "I don't know everything, but it looks like they all went there, all had blue bandanas, all had guns, it's not like they were not going to do something evil."

All were formally sentenced on August 28th, 2009. Simmons was given life with no possibility for parole for 25 years. Smith, Mundy, and Tolson received 20 year sentences. Attorneys said at the time that all pleaded guilty to avoid the death penalty, which they could have faced had they gone to trial.

Moore recognized that none apologized for their actions from the bench.

"And you would think that if someone murdered someone, that they would be remorseful. That they would say, 'I'm sorry,'" she said.

Moore did get a statement from Simmon's mother. Police said Simmons was the main triggerman in the shootings.

"She said 'I am sorry for the loss of your son,'" Moore said to me after the sentencings.

## Venus Ramey fires back

Occasionally one of my stories makes national news. On April 20th, a story about an 82-year-old woman who stood up to some metal thieves did just that, all because of who she used to be.

Venus Ramey won the Miss America pageant in 1944. After some years in Hollywood she returned to a farm in Eubank where in April 2007 she made headlines once again. There, when she was 82, when she says some people tried to get away with scrap metal, she confronted them at gunpoint.

When I got the call to do this story, I had no way to contact Mrs. Ramey. She wasn't listed in the phone book so I simply drove to where she lived, hoping I would get lucky with an interview. Sure enough, not long after I parked the WKYT SUV, here came Venus Ramey, walking down the road with the help of a walker.

She even showed me the revolver she used.

"And he said if you get out of my way, we'll leave. And I said, 'oh no you won't.' And I shot two shots in one of their tires," Ramey told me.

Only that wasn't enough...and she fired again with her "snub-nosed.38."

"I shot one (tire) and it wouldn't go down. I thought it would go 'woosh' and flatten but it didn't. They're not made that way, so I shot it again," she said.

Ramey with the gun in one hand and cell phone in the other called police. Officers arrived and charged a man with trespassing. Police say he took for the rap for others involved. The story later ended up on Fox News and other national news agencies. In fact, Fox News was going to air my entire story but on the same day a major airplane crash with continuous coverage pre-empted the story and only video of Ramey with the sound-bite made the news.

# CHAPTER 28

## Oh, Romeo!

I've said it before and I'll say it again. People love stories about animals. And a story I did in 2007 would eventually become fodder for a new state law.

On June 2007, abuse to the Pulaski County dog was caught on tape by a neighbor. Police told me it was one of the worst cases of animal abuse they had ever seen, caught on tape. The owner was arrested and charged after the video showed the dog being slammed to the ground, choked, and his dog house even dropped on top of him. About 6 months later we obtained that video and showed some of it, most of it being too disturbing to show on television.

Like the story about Roadie that aired several years before, the story garnered tremendous attention and interest. After the arrest Romeo was taken to the local animal shelter and it received hundreds of phone calls from people wanting to adopt the dog or just to make sure he was taken care of.

In October 2007 the case against the man accused of causing the abuse began working through the court system.

"People have been outraged and rightly so," the county attorney told me after one of the suspect appearances."I believe all they ask for is some kind of justice in the case."

The accused's defense was that the dog had bitten him twice and attempts to control him did not work. He ended up being convicted of animal cruelty charges and was sentenced to 4 months in jail.

"I lost my head. I lost my mind. All train of thought. What I did was inexcusable and I'm ashamed of it," he said during the trial.

About 7 months later the abuse case became the rallying call for a new state law that would make torture of a dog a cat a felony, punishable by 1 to 5 years in prison. It had the support of the state and national humane societies, based on the argument that many animal cruelty or abuse cases resulted in the accused only receiving a slap on the wrist instead of severe punishment. Most were charged only with misdemeanors.

Romeo remained in the care of a local vet until the legal case was resolved and currently resides on a Pulaski County farm. He made numerous appearances at the state capital as Romeo's Law worked its way through the legislative process and even attended ceremonial bill signing with the Governor.

# CHAPTER 29

## New equipment, new challenges.

A unique aspect of my job is that I am a one man show but also the equipment I use at WKYT is different from the camera and editing units used by the other reporters and videographers who work in Lexington.

When I was hired in 2003 I was given a DVC Pro ENG camera and what they called a tape-to-tape DVC Pro laptop editor. It was hardly a piece of equipment you would want to use in your lap, though, as it weighed more than 30 pounds! For five years I got used to editing tape to tape, meaning you would actually record from one tape to another in laying down audio tracks, then video "b-roll."

In June 2008 I was told that I was receiving a new camera and a new editor. The photographers at WKYT had recently been given new HD cameras that recorded on a disc instead of a tape. But because of the arrangement with the Somerset bureau, my gear would be different. It was different than anything else anyone knew how to use. Not only would I would be a one man band, I was the only one who knew how to use it!

The new camera and editor were HD capable but I shoot and edit in standard definition because I don't have any way to feed video in high definition. The camera uses what's called a P2 card and I tell people it's basically like a giant SD card that you have in your cameras or camcorders. The five P2 cards

I have each have 30 minutes of video and you can format or erase them thousands of times, without losing any quality.

The editor that I use was a whole new ball of wax. The first day of training I felt like the kid back in junior high math class who couldn't' understand how to do anything right. Frustrated was a minor statement. One of my bosses at WKYT sort of gave me some encouragement.

"Well, just go home and ask your (six-year -old) son how to use it," he joked.

After two full days of training from a Panasonic expert, I finally figured out how to use the editor. I'm still the only one at our station who knows how to edit on it! In most video editing systems, whether it's tape-to-tape linear or a non-linear computer based editing system that the ordinary Joe could figure out how to use on a lap-top, there's a simple system of laying down one video track, and at least two tracks of audio. On the old-fashioned tape-to-tape system, you would have three buttons on the console. If you wanted to lay down a track of video, you pushed the video button. If you wanted to put down natural sound, you would usually push the audio "2" button. If you're laying down a voice track or narrative, you push just the audio "1" button. If it's a sound-bite with the subject of the interview, you push both the audio "1" and video buttons. What is edited from one tape to another is based on what button you push for audio and video. And with other computer based non-linear systems I've used these buttons are there also…but in a computer based format.

With the P2 system I was using, these three buttons were not there so it was like I was learning how to re-invent the wheel all over again. With my editor, I would record my audio and video onto a timeline and then have to protect the audio track by pushing what's called the 'extra' button so I wouldn't erase it when I put my video down. It was confusing at first and again, it took several entire days of trial and error but finally I figured it out

When I was speaking to middle school students at a recent career day event, some of the kids seemed amazed when looking at the equipment. Their questions were all over their faces without even opening their mouths.

"How in the world do you know how to use all of this?" it was like they were asking.

The truth is, when I accepted the job as Southern Kentucky. Bureau Chief I had really never used a large professional TV camera before. I had no real experience in video editing. I didn't know how to interview someone on camera. Sure, I had TV production classes in college. But many times what's in the classroom is hardly enough to prepare you for real life. Honestly, I probably learned more in one month training at WKYT than I learned in 4 years in college!

New innovations in equipment is probably one reason there's more multi-media journalists being used today. The cameras are smaller; the systems more simple to use. One person can do it all. When I was speaking to the 7th and 8th graders, I had my camera, editor, and TVU transmitter unit all on the table. All of that is all I need to both record, edit, and feed my stories to the TV station. And it's all easy enough for one person to transport and use all by himself or herself.

Some of the students were amazed that I could set up my camera and shoot myself doing "stand-ups." That's the part of the story you see the reporter talking into the camera, usually at the beginning and or end of the piece, sometimes in the middle for what we call "the bridge."

It's actually very simple. With my camera I set it atop the tripod about my height, I turn the focus lens all the way to the right, make sure the zoom is wide, and turn the viewfinder monitor that's on the side of the camera facing toward the front so I can see myself. Older cameras didn't have the side viewfinder so I used to have to record my standup, then rewind the segment and play it back in the regular viewfinder to watch myself and make sure I was in frame. And in focus. Sometimes I would have to do it several times if I cut off my head or there was too much headroom or if I was out of focus.

# CHAPTER 30

## Who stole Jesus?

Now that I have your attention, no one actually stole Jesus, but a doll of baby Jesus in a nativity scene. This was my story on Christmas Eve, 2008. And what made the story even better was that instead of interviewing the adult victims, I focused everything on their kids and only used the interviews from them in the package.

"Who would stoop down so low? I would have felt a whole lot better if it was something else," one of the children said.

Not only was the baby Jesus stolen, but the thieves ripped Christmas lights from another house. The Pulaski County attorney was also a victim! Ironically, he was the one who found the stolen baby Jesus and returned it to the family.

"I went into my room and said, 'thank you Lord, thank you Lord!" one of the kids said to me.

The family had a great message about the whole ordeal and said they actually used the "tragedy" to teach their children that Christmas should not be about material things. Police ended up finding the grinches who stole baby Jesus and it seems like because of the widespread publicity the story received, they ended up receiving a pretty harsh sentence, and not a slap on the wrist.

# CHAPTER 31
## Ice storm 2009

Weather is a huge part of the news. Some may argue it's too much of the newscast, others could say it's not enough. And some hate it when special weather announcements interrupt their favorite TV show.

Kentucky is in a part of the country where we have all four seasons and sometimes these season run into each other and sometimes you just never know what the weather is going to be like. As I'm writing this right now, on a cold Saturday in late October, it feels more like January outside than October. You never know what's going to happen and that's probably why weather is such a huge part of not just what meteorologists do…but what all of us reporters do.

"When in doubt, lead with weather," my news director has said.

In January 2009 the weather reared its ugly head and our weather people earned their pay in a major way. A thick coat of ice covered parts of central and south-central Kentucky. Parts of Boyle, Lincoln and surrounding counties lost electricity for days and people camped out in hotels, shelters, or just wherever they could find a warm place to stay. This affected me personally because we also lost electricity.

Since my father-in-law was in a Lexington hospital having open heart surgery, my family made the decision to stay in a hotel up there until the power was restored.

My story for nearly a week was about the same. People dealing with and surviving through the ice storm. Crews from other states were brought in by the electric utilities to help restore power. Those guys worked 16 to 18 hour shifts, usually surviving on three to four hours of sleep a night, to restore the miles of electric lines taken down by the weight of the frozen H20.

"It's really dangerous. The trees are bad. I wouldn't recommend anyone trying to come out and clean your yard yet," one electric crewman told me while working in Stanford.

# CHAPTER 32
## Sports

In any given newscast, you have the news, weather and sports. It's the same in any market. In some places, the weather isn't a big deal. In other markets sports isn't either. But in Kentucky, weather and sports are absolutely huge. And basketball in particular, *UK Basketball,* is enormously important.

For several years leading up to 2009, UK basketball had lost some of its luster. But that all changed on April 1 when John Calipari was introduced as the new head basketball coach. And I had a part of the news coverage that introduced him.

I drive a news vehicle home every night and at the time I was in a 2002 Ford Escape. It needed some work so I just happened to schedule some repairs on April 1 at Paul Miller Ford in Lexington. I was in the waiting room as the TV had live coverage, on WKYT, of Calipari's news conference and being introduced as the UK coach. I actually didn't know what story I would be working on that day but it soon became apparent that Calapari's hiring wouldn't just be the number one news story that day, it was about the ONLY news story that day. Multiple reporters were doing all kinds of different angles focusing on the new coach and since I was at the place where Calipari would be become a major spokesman, my producer told me to just do a story there. Talk about killing two birds with one stone. Wait for the car to be fixed…interview the people there!

So I went around the dealership and interviewed a few salesman about Calipari. They told me how previous coaches were great ambassadors for the car lot. Not only would Calipari do commercials about Paul Miller, he would also drive one of their cars or trucks.

"It's about time we had an ambassador not only to the school but for the community," one of the dealers told me.

I actually had two stories about Calipari that day and the second one happened all because of a four-second statement he made during the introductory news conference.

"I love Dunkin Donuts. Dunkin Donuts is my thing," Calipari said.

Because he said that and because of who owned the local franchise, a story all about the donut business and the "Calipari connection" was ordered. So I delivered.

The Dunkin Donuts on Broadway in Lexington was owned by former UK Coach Rick Pitino and some former Wildcats and its manager was Collier Mills, whose brother Cameron played for the Cats in the 90s.

"Just to hear him say, 'Dunkin Donuts' in the conference, without any hesitation, was exciting for us," Mills told me.

I ended the story this way: "Pitino and Calipari will no doubt have a strong rivalry on the court, yet in Dunkin Donuts it appears they're both on the same team. In Lexington, Phil Pendleton, WKYT 27 Newsfirst."

I was equally excited about John Calipari's hiring because I knew what was good for Kentucky basketball was good for the "Official UK Station" in WKYT.

In 2005 I was fortunate enough to be on two crews following the Cats in the SEC and NCAA tournaments. But

I hadn't had the opportunity to cover them anymore, partly because since 2005 Kentucky wasn't as much of a factor in the post season, so WKYT didn't send as large a crew. And I was basically told that I probably wouldn't be called upon to travel to a tournament unless Kentucky was in a Final Four. And that happened in 2011.

I'll go ahead and jump ahead to then. I was actually on the crew list that was going to help cover the Cats in the 2010 Final Four if they were to make it. But they didn't. A year later, the prospects of Kentucky making it to the Final Four were slim. Kentucky had a decent year, but even in the NCAA tournament their road looked extremely difficult. If they were to make the finals in Houston, they would have to beat Number one seed Ohio State…then possibly face North Carolina in the Elite Eight. They did just that and sure enough moments after the victory I got a text message from my assignment editor that was pure gold.

"I think you're going," was all that it said.

And sure enough about an hour later, my boss called me and asked me to tell him exactly how my name appeared on my driver's license.

"Phillip A. Pendleton, what's this for… an airline ticket?" I asked.

"Yes, to Houston," was all he said.

So about four days later myself and a handful of other reporters, photographers and sports folk boarded a plane in Lexington to Houston for the 2011 Final Four. We got in late that Thursday night and our day started early Friday morning.

Anchor Amber Philpot and me set out early that Friday morning to interview fans. When reporters or one-man bands go on trips on like this, it's usually to do just do fans pieces but in any trip with a crew the size of ours, you do a little bit of everything.

Because we flew and didn't rent cars our only way of transportation around Houston was by cab. I believe by the time we left all of us had probably spent several hundred dollars in cab fare and there's one cabbie that has a special place in my heart that I'll get to later.

The story that Amber and I did focused on some sisters who traveled as college students to the Final Four in 1998 and then back as working adults in 2011. Later that day I did a package all by myself on the CBS Sports crew putting together the show that is the Final Four. It was so cool doing my stand-ups on the floor of the massive Reliant Stadium, then shooting video of the practice and the surroundings that would soon be the focus of the college basketball world the next three days.

That night Amber and I shot a story about fans at a pep rally/concert but shortly after getting back to the SAT truck, I noticed I didn't have my microphone bag. I had left it in the cab!

I was frantic. I had a stick mic, a lapel mic and several mic cords in that bag and honestly I didn't think I'd ever see it again. I don't know how many cab drivers there are in Houston but I'm sure there are thousands and the chances of seeing the same guy again was probably next to nil. But sure enough about an hour later I got a phone call on my cell phone..all because of another very important thing I also had in that fanny pack—a business card.

The cabbie had found my fanny back when cleaning out his car and called the number on the business card.

"Hey…this is (don't remember his name) and I have something of yours you left in my cab," he said.

"Oh man, you are an answer to prayer!" I said.

Despite being on the other side of Houston, and Houston is a huge city, he agreed to drive all the way back to me to give me back my bag and equipment. I agreed to pay him $20. For as long as it took him to get back, he probably spent all of that in gasoline alone, because it took him more than an hour to get back to me. It was something he didn't have to do. But it saved my company hundreds of dollars because I'm sure it would have been very expensive to replace the equipment I would have lost.

As I said being a member of a TV news crew on a tournament trip means you work, then you work some more. Each day started at about 8 a.m. and didn't' end until well after the 11p.m. news. By the time we cleaned up and put everything away it was usually well after midnight. And we usually didn't have time for supper so we were usually eating dinner about the 11 p.m. news, which meant by the time we got back to the hotel it was pushing 1 a.m. But I loved every minute of it.

Saturday was the first day of the semifinal games and Kentucky was to play Connecticut in the first game, about six that night. Our chief photographer, Amber and I traveled to an event downtown that had a battle of the pep bands contest and various games for the fans that we made into a story. I also edited both my stories and Amber's and ran a live camera for the anchors. Sometimes I was just a gopher, getting whatever anyone needed.

Saturday night the game came and Kentucky lost. Afterwards I shot for Jennifer Palumbo getting reaction from fans and helped edit the post game coverage. Then I got behind a camera and shot the anchors giving the news of the big loss. I thought it was interesting how the signs on Reliant Stadium had a completely different meaning while saying the same thing after the loss. The signs said "The road ends here." Going to the tournament, it was positive. Wow, the road ends with Kentucky in the Final Four. How exciting! But after the loss, Kentucky's season was over. Their road had ended. Still, it was a great trip and despite getting ready to head home on Sunday, I had a trip of a lifetime. And something was about to happen while heading home that made returning after just one game, and not after the championship game, even sweeter.

After UK lost, our news director back in Lexington began changing our flights to return home on Sunday instead of Tuesday after the title game. In hurried fashion, something happened and I ended up getting put on some kind of mistaken stand-by. Long story short, when we were checking into the gate, my name did not show up on the boarding list. It was actually a mistake the airline made and they told me that unless someone else was willing to give up their seat, I would have to find a later flight back. The sweet part was that no one did give up their seat, and I earned some big bucks because of it!

Since the airline clearly was at fault they told me that they were going to pay me $800 for their mistake. I had to fly into Louisville because no more flights were available that day to Lexington. The payout was for the inconvenience. So I had to wait around for several hours to fly home, all the while extremely thankful for the big check in my wallet. Good things come to those that wait!

I was also on the crew list for the 2012 Final Four when Kentucky finally did win it all, but a last minute change because of another crew member becoming ill took me off the list. And here's to hoping that I'll also be on additional Final Fours in years to come! .

# CHAPTER 33

## Multiple missing persons

2009 was a big year for news, as most years are, but there was a common theme among many stories in the second half of that year. Missing people seemed to dominate the stories and many of the mysteries came from the same part of the state. All in the area I frequently cover.

On October 15th of that year Charles Randolph, 55, disappeared. His family says he was last seen getting into a white SUV from his home on Cochran Road. in the rural part of Kings Mountain in Casey County near the Lincoln County line. His relatives told me that they feared he may have been running with the "wrong crowd." They said there were signs of a struggle in his front yard as a necklace was found in the grass. It was unusual they said because he left his dog, his truck and medicine that he would have wanted to take with him if he was planning on being gone for several days.

"He would do anything for anybody. And he was too good hearted. And that may be what happened. He was too good hearted with people," his sister Freda Elmore told me on October 27th, 2009.

The missing person case has been under investigation ever since by the Casey County Sheriff's Office. Deputies insist they don't have physical evidence of foul play but haven't ruled it out either.

"I feel something is definitely not right," Deputy Chad Weddle said during a search of a pond on Nov. 19th, 2009. "As far as any factual information, saying foul play has happened, we don't really have that yet."

I went back to Randolph's family's house on Christmas Eve that year for a remembrance piece, knowing his absence would be tough during what is usually a joyous time of the year.

"Tonight we're having Mom's Christmas and it's going to be hard," sister Freda Elmore told me.

It was about that time that police revealed they did find and impound a white SUV Randolph may have been seen getting into. A court ordered that it be tested for DNA samples and that was finally done in February of 2013. Results have not been made public.

Police did say in April of 2010 that they believed Randolph did not leave home on his own, but relatives didn't know what to make of that. Since his absence, police have searched several ponds and there have been areas of land dug up. But no sign of the man. In May 2011, close to Memorial Day, believing their brother was dead, his sisters put up a grave marker in their church cemetery.

"It would be nice if we had a body, if we ever find him. That's what we want to do," Elmore told me.

"It's good to have this here. To be able to come and remember him. But we know his body is not here. That is hard. We don't have closure," said sister Shirley Austin.

Then in November of that year, Jeffrey Kevin Price disappeared. He was last seen at his workplace at Somerset Harwood, just north of Somerset. His burned-up truck was found later that night next to a nearby pond. Over the next several weeks I ran numerous updates on the hunt for him, many times interviewing Price's father, Jeff.

"I've come to the conclusion, yes, that someone has killed my son, yes," he told me in an update that aired on November 27th, 2009. Price's family had their Thanksgiving dinner that year without Kevin at the table. How horrible it must have been not just knowing that Kevin was missing, but not knowing what happened or why.

Price's family would find some closure when his body was found a few days after that Thanksgiving in a burn pit on Strawberry Road in a very rural and remote section of Pulaski County, several miles from Somerset. And a great distance from where he was last seen. The area was known for ATV riding, hunting, fishing but also partying and illegal drug activity.

Police still haven't said exactly how Price died, but they have ruled it a murder.

"I don't think anybody had any hate towards him, and if they did, they did a good job of hiding it," his father, Jeff told me on Nov. 30th just before his son's funeral.

500 people attended Price's funeral visitation and the Pulaski Funeral Home was also packed for the final services.

"I expected all of those because I know my son was loved. I know however, whichever way my son died, he wasn't to go like this. He was loved by too many friends," his father told me just before the funeral on Dec. 8, 2009. Price was buried next to his mother, who lost her battle with cancer a few years before.

Police said they had interviewed hundreds of people but no suspects have ever been named.

In February of 2010, Mr. Price spent hundreds of dollars of his own money in paying for a billboard asking for the public's help. Each year on the anniversary and sometimes more frequently, he puts similar messages on the flashing sign. Price told me that the "Justice for Kevin" message would flash more than a thousand times and that it would be seen by thousands of drivers each day on an electronic billboard that changed messages frequently.

"You don't give up. Just try to hold your head up and don't let this kind of thing drag you down," he said in a Feb. 8, 2010 story.

In September 2011 Price's grandmother agreed to a rare interview, also wanting viewers to see her "Justice for Kevin" sticker she put on the back of her car.

"It's very hard for me to say I've got two grandsons because one is gone," Lela Whitaker told me on Sept. 26th, 2011.

Both the Randolph case in Casey County and Price murder in Pulaski County have rewards. Randolph's family has $10,000 to be paid to the person or persons who provide his whereabouts and the reward in the Price murder mystery is more than $20,000. Price's father told me in November 2013 that the reward is larger now but he did not want the specific amount released.

"We want to make sure (the tipster) is serious," he said.

Price has also put flyers in storefronts, signs on cars and advertisements throughout town.

"Make sure no one out there forgets that I've got a son that's been murdered. No one is going to stop until it's solved," Price said. He hoped seeing all the signs of the unsolved case would get to the killers.

"And each of them will have to look at those things and know that we're looking for you and we're going to find you, and we will get you, " Price told me, looking and pointing into my camera lense the entire time.

Both cases, in addition to similar cases of missing persons nearby in Taylor and Marion Counties, have developed a lot of contacts for me that, to be honest, I wish I didn't have to have. All of these families have deal with tremendous pain but they realize the importance of the news media in getting the word out and reminding people of the unsolved cases. Because Pulaski, Casey, Taylor and Marion Counties are all in "my area," I'm usually the only reporter for WKYT that covers these stories. And I can't wait until these families have the closure they're looking for and I get to report the final outcomes.

# CHAPTER 34
## The jailhouse interview

What I'm about to write about I must admit was the whole reason for wanting to write this book. I've had a lot of interesting stories in the ten years I've been at WKYT but I think the interview I did on June 11, 2010 wasn't just the best interview, it was probably one of the most interesting and bizarre stories I did. And just the case of being honest, or somewhat honest, could have been the one reason the judge ended up throwing the book at these two people.

On June 11th I did a story about a rash of burglaries all over Corbin. Later I found out the pair arrested also broke into many other places in Williamsburg. The two arrested, James Day and James Sprinkles agreed to what we call in the business, "the jailhouse interview."

The jailhouse interview is just that. The media comes in and talks to the person accused in jail. It's something that before I got into television news I never did. I never tried it in radio or when I worked for the newspaper. And I don't think I even attempted one at WKYT until years after I watched one by one of our competitors. But over the past years, some of the producers at WKYT and WYMT have nicknamed me "the king of the jailhouse interview." Now I don't say that to boost my ego or say I'm better than anyone else. It's not because of anything I have done. It's because of what many of these suspects have told me!

It seems like I've been able to get some of the most memorable confessions or "Heck, no I didn't do it!" stories from behind bars. What I got on June 11, 2010 was a confession and I bet now that both Mr. Day and Mr. Sprinkles probably wish they had kept their mouths shut that day.

"There's a difference between justice and righteous justice," one of the two told me from jail. That was righteous justice."

"Even if it hurts somebody?" I asked

"If it has to," he replied.

Day and Sprinkles were talking about their crime spree at four businesses in the downtown Corbin area over a two-week period in late May and early June 2010. But there could have been more because police told me they also confessed to another break-in they hadn't known about.

Both men told me from jail they broke into all the businesses to get money to help Day's fiancé with a medical condition. Yet they also admitted to consuming a lot of the alcohol they also stole during the heists.

"Yes sir…I'm still waking from it," Day said, and he and Sprinkles broke in wild laughter.

Both men later apologized during the interview. Well, they *sort of* said they were sorry.

"I'm sorry for bothering the community. Bothering the community. But no, I'd do it again," they said.

And as for Day's fiancé? Well, she broke up with him after he was arrested.

The story got a lot better two months later. But not for the suspects. During a court appearance the circuit judge recused himself because he learned he was also a victim of the pair's crime spree!

"I'm about to recuse because you stole a knife from me and I want it back," Hon. Dan Ballou said during what would have been a routine court appearance for Day and Sprinkles in Whitley Circuit Court.

It turns out that Judge Ballou was among the numerous victims the two stole from during their two week crime spree. Ballou was an indirect victim because a knife of his was among the items taken when the Office of Probation and Parole was burglarized. Ballou's wife worked there and his knife was apparently in her desk.

"This little bitty thing, a $5 pocket knife and it says Marines on it. I want it back. Get them out of my face!" Judge Ballou told the bailiff.

That bailiff apparently couldn't get the suspects out of the courtroom fast enough. He kept yelling at them as they were leaving.

"Hurry up! Go! Now I want my knife back and I mean it. Only a $5 knife but I want it back," Judge Ballou says to them.

WKYT aired almost the entire encounter between the two. I wasn't in the courtroom when it happened, but we were able to buy the courtroom video. Video of court proceedings are available through the Kentucky Open Records laws but they're not cheap. Each tape or disc costs $20. But that story was worth every penny.

I didn't cover the final outcome of their case but I heard that both received a harsher penalty than they probably would have received had their case not received so much publicity, mostly because that jailhouse interview the two did where they basically bragged about their crime spree. Just think, those two will spend more time in prison and won't be released early, all because of what they told me in jail, what thousands of viewers saw.

# CHAPTER 35

## The Relief Trip

As I've said before a part of this job that I've really grown to love over the years is being able to travel. And in 2011, then again in 2013, I was presented with several opportunities to follow groups from Kentucky assisting those in states devastated from tornadoes.

In April 2011, a series of tornadoes hit parts of the southeast, including Alabama. The twisters were more than a mile wide in some places and entire neighborhoods were wiped out. I witnessed the aftermath of the destruction first hand when I followed several groups from Kentucky who traveled to the Tuscaloosa area in early May 2011. One of those was a church group from Somerset. On May 3 of that year a group spent a rainy day in a store parking lot collecting supplies that they would deliver to a church in Alabama.

I just happened to be at the store when I noticed the group and decided to make what they were doing my story for the day. The minister of Oak Hill Baptist Church, Gary Phelps, said he had family and friends in the Birmingham area and quickly learned of the needs.

"He told me the needs he had," Phelps said of a conversation with a fellow pastor in the area. "(He said he) had over 1,000 kids that needed school supplies and they tarps over houses and things like that."

Among the things the group took down were flashlights because weeks after the tornado hit, many areas were still without electricity and some were still living in homes without power. For many, a flashlight was the difference in getting around at night, or stubbing your toe over and over again.

Later that day as I was putting the story together, I talked with my news director about going. In two hours time I discovered two other groups from Kentucky in Alabama and made plans for a quick day and a half trip to the Birmingham area to cover Kentucky relief efforts.

The next day I left my house in my WKYT Toyota Corolla packed with gear and a suitcase and set out for central Alabama. My first assignment was covering the Christian Appalachian Project clearing trees and debris away and then I followed some electric workers restoring power.

The next day I met up with Phelps and his crew putting tarps on houses and doing basic handy-man work.

The church group from Somerset actually had to "smuggle" me and my gear in because of the increased security in the Tuscaloosa area. Police were only allowing residents and relief workers in because of looters and a news crew from Kentucky would not have met their clearance rules!

So the church group met me in a parking lot, I put my gear in the back of the truck hidden under supplies and rode in the front seat while seeing the devastation first hand. Seeing what an EF-4 or EF-5 tornado can do is like witnessing a toddler walk through a town built of popsicle sticks. Hardly anything is left. That tornado killed more than 60 people across Alabama and many were left starting over.

The Somerset group said people in the Alabama neighborhood were overwhelmed by their kindness.

"One lady, her name was April. She had three kids in her car. We filled the car up and a two and three year old had to get on top of it," one of the church volunteers told me.

My coverage of the tornado relief almost never made it to air because of equipment failure! When you're a one man show with one camera, and it breaks, you're pretty much finished. That happened as I was about to leave Tuscaloosa for the Birmingham, Ala. CBS affiliate where I would edit and feed my video.

I had just left the Somerset group and was driving through town looking for a good place to shoot my stand-ups. I found an ideal place with a lot of destruction in the background. I popped the trunk, got out, set up my tripod and got the camera out. I turned it on. Nothing. No power. I figured the battery was probably just dead so I put on another batter. Still no power. I tried another one. Nothing. The camera was dead. Luckily the only thing I had not shot were my stand-ups so I was still able to salvage 95% of the story.

I drove to the TV station edited my story and started heading for home. But on the way back, my cell phone rang with news of another assignment that would involve me covering a historic event.

For some in Washington, D.C. covering The President of the United States is an every day thing. But for a one man band in Kentucky, it's a once in a lifetime opportunity. That happened to me on a warm, sunny day on the first Friday in May, 2011.

But without a camera what as I to do?

My producer called me and told me that President Barack Obama was headed to Fort Campbell, Kentucky to personally congratulate those who had taken out Osama bin Laden. "SEAL Team Six" was at Fort Campbell but the President also wanted to thank the many other soldiers for their efforts in the War on Terror.

I was told to head toward Fort Campbell, spend the night at a Hampton Inn near the base and over the President's remarks the next day. Security is extremely tight with a U.S. Presidential visit, and I had to be at the base hours before the remarks. President Obama was scheduled to address the troops at 4 p.m. but we had to be at Fort Campbell at 9 a.m. to begin the security process. I still have the White House Press Corp. badge I received that day, which is something every media member receives, whether you're covering the President at the White House at another location. Pretty cool.

As I said before, I didn't have a camera and covering The President as a one man band was going to be a huge challenge. Luckily WYMT was sending their SAT truck and another reporter and they had an extra camera that I was going to be able to use. Hours after finally passing through security, we set up on a stage 50 or so yards away from where Obama would address soldiers in a hot airplane hanger. The President was to start speaking at 4 p.m., and I was to go live at 5 p.m. The problem was that the President was delayed and his speech didn't end until 4:40. That meant I had 20 minutes to write my script and edit my package. All the while working in a 100 degree building with dozens of other media members scrambling around me. Talk about pressure. Here you area covering one of the most important people *in the world,* and you're given only minutes to put together not just the biggest story of the day, but likely of the entire year.

Because of the time constraints, I basically just jumped in front of the camera with hundreds of troops milling around The President in the background and went live, reporting on what he had just talked moments before. Almost immediately after Obama left, the army base officials told the media to leave, so I only had about 30 minutes to edit my 6 p.m. story. It was a whirlwind day but an amazing opportunity to cover.

And just a few weeks later I was called on to cover another event in Joplin, Missouri.

On May 22, 2011, an EF-5 tornado cut a path of destruction six miles long and a mile wide. According to The Joplin Globe, 8,000 structures were destroyed, 142 lives were lost and more than 1,000 were injured. Like in Alabama, Kentuckians were among the many who answered the call to help.

A group of people traveled with the Christian Appalachian Project to deliver supplies and help clean up the area. I covered them delivering a tractor-trailer load of everything from toilet paper to bottled water. Many of the people I spoke with said they wanted to help because they knew the victims went from having everything to having nothing. In just seconds.

About a year later, I went back to Joplin for a special story on how the town rebuilt. The point of the story was to show how the Missouri town recovered and the lessons learned from it. My news director thought it was a good idea because it would show Kentuckians who had just suffered from tornados in Laurel, Morgan, and Menifee counties and other areas 'how it was done.'

One of the areas I went to was Kentucky Avenue in Joplin. I interviewed a family who had to start over, with a brand new home, new possessions, new everything. Like many families, an interior storm shelter was a no-brainer.

"It's not the expense, it's the piece of mind," the resident told me of the $4,000 expenditure that was more or less a metal closet designed to withstand 200 mph winds and anything it could throw at you. The best piece of advice from surviving a tornado? People told me it was patience and working together.

On May 20th, 2013 an EF-5 tornado hit Moore, Oklahoma killing 23 people with its winds of more than 200 miles per hour. Once again we learned of groups from Kentucky traveling there to help and once again I was called upon to travel there for relief stories. One of my producers came with another nickname for me. "Tornado Phil." And once there, I found myself right smack in the middle of another storm!

I arrived in Moore on May 31 with plans to cover a group of Red Cross volunteers from Lexington doing relief work in feeding people and cleaning debris. That afternoon there were storms in the forecast so I was told to get there by 3 p.m. because by 4 all the volunteers would be indoors. So I didn't have a large window to get my work done.

This was my first trip I was able to use the TVU transmitter that WKYT had been using for about a year. For years, about the only way to feed back video professionally was through a SAT truck or a microwave transmission. But the TVU is an amazing piece of equipment that's in the form of a back pack. You simply hook audio and video cables to your editor, push a button, and in about 10 seconds, the editors at WKYT can see and hear your package. Inside the TVU are a bunch of cell phones and it uses all of them at once to feed the audio and video. The quality isn't quite as good as using a SAT or microwave truck and it isn't in high definition, but if there's a good strong 4G signal, you're not going to tell much of a difference. Since been given my own TVU unit in the fall of 2012, I've been able to work from just about anywhere, even from home. As long as there's a good strong cell phone signal, I can work in almost any environment. Some days I've been able to edit and feed my stories from my kitchen table. Other days I work out of the front seat of my car.

I arrived in Moore about 3 p.m. and quickly interviewed a Red Cross volunteer who told me of helping people and witnessing the horrendous devastation. I remember him taking me to an elementary school where seven children were killed and where seven wooden crosses were built as a makeshift memorial to them.

Not long after editing and feeding the story from the front seat of my car, I quickly drove to an another elementary school where a group from Lincoln County, Kentucky was delivering supplies. Not long after arriving there my phone wrong and it was my boss.

"Phil, this is Robert and I have Chris Bailey (WKYT's chief meteorologist) here with me, where are you?" my news director asked.

"I'm parked in a school lot just outside Oklahoma City. I'm really not sure where I am," I said. That was the truth. I had used by GPS to get me around the area and I really didn't know geographically where I was, but while talking to him I quickly noticed the skies turning very dark. Not just dark like we're used to in Kentucky. The skies over Oklahoma that late-afternoon were almost *black.*

"Hey, Phil, this is Chris. We wanted to call you because the area you're in is about to be hit by a storm system that's like nothing I've ever seen before and it could get bad," he warned.

Robert and Chris called me first because they wanted to make sure I was safe and secondly because what was about to happen was literally about to become part of my story. I quickly finished up the interview with the Lincoln County people and got back in the car to head for my hotel. I was about 30 miles from the hotel Robert had booked me in and I wasn't sure where the storm was coming from or when it would arrive. But from the look of sky above me, it was coming quickly.

During most of the drive to the hotel it never rained but it looked like the sky was literally about to fall. Chicken Little needed to get indoors and get indoors quick!

By the time I got to the hotel, it started raining. I listened to the coverage on the radio and before long the announcers were talking of seeing twisters. Most of it was occurring west of Oklahoma City and I didn't know it at the time but I was about 30 to 40 miles east of there and nowhere near the danger. But the tornadoes that touched down that night would end up being some of the most severe and unique ever seen in the history of weather forecasting.

I got back to the hotel and edited my package that night focusing on the Kentucky relief efforts. But since the new storm was developing as I was working, my producers at WKYT wanted me to record a set of stand-up ins and outs talking about the breaking weather situation. Honestly, it wasn't safe enough to set up outside and I was afraid the winds would probably blow down my camera and tripod. Plus it was raining so hard that even with raingear on my camera, I didn't think there was any way to keep my gear dry. Keep in mind, I was by myself! My wife thought it was funny that the anchors kept talking about the "crew" in Oklahoma during the storm when the "crew" was simply me!

I set up my camera on the tripod in my hotel room with the desk, lamp and closed curtain behind me. I basically opened up my package with me looking into the camera talking about how I was in Oklahoma City, safe in a hotel room while there was news of devastation taking place just west of me. I felt like the correspondents in Baghdad hotels during the first Gulf

War in 1990, reporting while bombs could be heard going off in the background!

It was actually hard putting my piece together because everyone and their uncle was texting or calling me. They were watching the national coverage and they knew I was out there and they called me or texted me to make sure I was OK.

"Phillip (that's what my wife calls me), Mom called and wants to know if we need to activate the prayer chain at church," my wife asked.

I almost laughed but in reality they had a right to be scared for me. Two years before dozens were killed in a similar storm in Alabama, more than 160 perished in Joplin and just weeks before almost 30 died in a similar storm just a few miles away. And it seemed like it was happening again.

In fact some at the hotel told me that the hotel next door was destroyed in another round of twisters that hit the area in the late 1990s.

I fed my story and since I hadn't eaten a bite since that morning, I drove to get a burger at a local fast food eatery. While driving there and back I don't think I've ever seen a harder rain. It was like that seen in *Forrest Gump* where he talks about the rain coming down in every direction possible.

I ate and went to bed late and every so often I woke up in the middle of the night to hear it rain. I rained and rained and rained. You could hear the rain all night long. I managed to still get a fairly good night's sleep and the next morning it was still raining hard.

The next morning, while eating breakfast, I watched the local coverage of the aftermath of what happened the night before. There were flooded streets, destroyed homes and power lines down all over El Reno, Oklahoma. The meteorologists on the local Oklahoma City stations kept talking about a 'rain-wrapped tornado' and many of them said in their dozens of years of forecasting, they had never seen anything like it. The 2.6 mile-wide twister ended up being the widest ever recorded. That's why Chris Bailey had called me the afternoon before, because he predicted something historic was about to happen. And there I was, in the middle of weather history being made. And later that day, I was able to report on a survival story that made national news that had a strong Kentucky connection.

After getting ready on Saturday, June 1, I was going to focus my work that day on a group of police officers doing storm clean up in Moore. But that group's arrival was delayed by the storm the night before. I found myself needing a new story and it didn't take too long to find it.

One of the stories that made both the local and national news on June 1 was of a car of storm chasers who survived the tornado picking up their car and literally tossing it down. Inside that was freelance photojournalist Brad Reynolds from Whitesburg, Ky. He had been working for The Weather Channel and was in a SUV tracking the storm near El Reno when the "Tornado Hunt 2013" car was picked up and tossed down. No one inside was seriously hurt.

"I remember it was really quiet and then I was holding on to anything I could, trying to brace myself for the fall," Reynolds told me in the story that aired on June 1, 2013.

All three in the car had their seat belts on and all walked away. While they were lucky, three others in another car were not. The storm also picked up another car of veteran storm chasers and the three inside died from their injuries.

I would spend one more day in Oklahoma focusing on a church group from Lincoln County who drove to Moore to simply feed local residents and I highlighted a group of first responders who went to Oklahoma simply to help police officers there who had not had time to take care of their own property. So after a 1,200 mile round trip that lasted about three and a half days, I was able to feed back seven different packages all focusing on Kentucky connections or relief in Oklahoma. It was because of the satisfaction of reporting such heartwarming stories of people helping or surviving in such terrible situations, that whenever I get the call to travel to these places, it's a call I usually have no trouble in answering!

# CHAPTER 36
## Aleigha

Perhaps no story will break your heart more than having to report on the death of a child. On Halloween night 2011, 5-year-old Aleigha Duvall was trick or treating near her rural Clinton County home and was crossing the street when she was hit by a truck. She died the next day at UK Hospital. And the following day, I went to her elementary school where her principal and teacher opened up to me about losing their little "princess."

"She would give you a hug every day. She would tell you she loved you," said Jackie Frey, Aleigha's teacher.

The stories we told were highlighted by pictures of Aleigha in a princess outfit. And on the sign outside the school, it read "We miss our little princess."

"She was a princess Halloween night. And now she is an angel," her uncle told me during a balloon lift held in her memory several days after her death.

All the kids at her school decorated balloons and let them go into the sky at the same time. I think the greatest thing about that story wasn't watching the hundreds of colored balloons fill the sparkling blue November sky that day, but instead it was listening to all the kids' oohs and aahs, and shouts of "wow!" as the balloons were lifted up.

"It's been so inspiring to see how many people who loved this little girl as much as we did," her uncle told me.

This was one story where people pushed for something good to come from something so bad.

"We're convinced that God will show us why this happened someday. So much good can come from this," I was told.

Her family wanted to highlight the dangers of trick or treating and at first tried to drum up support for a state law that would require children to wear reflective tape or markings on their Halloween costumes. That later became a resolution by the Albany City Council. The recommendation asked that parents put stripes on either the costume's arms or legs, similar to what is on road construction vests.

Aleigha's mother said it didn't bother her that the resolution did not become a state law. She said she was encouraged that it at least raised awareness.

A year later I interviewed Aleigha's mother for the first time. She told me that in the year since her daughter died, she learned that sometimes it takes the worst of times to bring out the best in others.

"It's just a reminder of how precious life is. If we can help somebody else and make it better that's what we want to do. That's what she (Aleigha) would want," Misty Hickman told me in October 2012.

Hickman said in addition to the reflective tape on costumes, she made it a point to constantly ask drivers to slow down and to try to keep an extra eye for children who may dart in front of cars.

"Maybe we can prevent another family from going through what we have experienced," she said.

# CHAPTER 37

## It kept getting worse.

On June 14, 2012, I was heading south on US 27, thinking I would start my day at the Somerset bureau. But I received a phone call telling me that a number of people were looking for a missing woman in Russell County.

So I turned around and headed south on US 127 into Jamestown, where sure enough in the parking lot of a local chicken restaurant, a large group of people had mobilized themselves into looking for Sarah Hart, 31, a pharmacist, wife, and mother of three small children.

Hart and her sister had been up for an early morning jog when Sarah started feeling sick and decided to head back to their car to wait for her sister. Only when the sister came back, Sarah was nowhere to be found. Her sister knew something was wrong. Later that day we would all discover just how bad it was, and how all the news just kept getting worse.

When I reported on the story at noon that day, it was simply how state police and local emergency officials were trying to locate the 31 year old. Sarah Hart worked in Mt. Vernon and lived in Russell Springs. Her father was a minister and Sarah had been working with the Vacation Bible School that week at their church.

People started going door to door with flyers. It was broadcast on the local radio stations. Dozens, if not hundreds, were trying to find her. Helicopters searched from the air.

Not long after my noon story hit the air, word of a tragic find filled the area. I was heading down US 127 when I started notice traffic starting to back up. I pulled over into the grass and then an ambulance sped and rushed to a stop. Moments later people started running, then reaching for one another, then holding each other. There was crying and wailing. Something terrible had just happened, or had just been discovered.

What happened was the body of the woman was found underneath some heavy brush. Sarah Hart was dead, but why? What happened? Was it a crime? Did she get sick and collapse under a tree?

At first I thought it would come back a natural cause death because Mrs. Hart did complain of being sick and I thought maybe she had a stroke or some other kind of medical condition brought on by her strenuous run.

During that day's 5 and 6 p.m. newscasts, my reports were simply focused on a woman running who got sick, went missing and was found dead, and how police were investigating. In a nutshell, that's all we knew and all we could report.

"We would treat it as a crime scene, until we process it as such. Take our time and make sure we don't leave out anything," Kentucky State Police spokesperson Billy Gregory told me that afternoon.

Later that day, after I posted my story I was driving home when my phone rang.

"Phil, this is Billy Gregory (with State Police), did you get our advisory?" he asked.

"Well, I'm not sure, which one?" I asked.

"About the arrest," he said.

"The arrest.? What arrest? What crime?" I asked, dumbfounded. Was this about the missing woman in Russell County?

"Do you mean she was....killed? I asked.

"Yes, we've made an arrest in her murder," Gregory said.

So on the 11 p.m. news that night my colleagues reported that Sarah Hart was kidnapped, murdered, and her body was thrown under a tree. Horrible.

What police figured out was that Christopher Allman, 28, on his way to work at a local auto repair shop, when he allegedly grabbed Hart and strangled her before leaving her body under some brush beside US 127 in Jamestown. He then took some of her belongings. As I stated earlier, news about what happened to her kept getting worse.

During the autopsy it was discovered that Hart was pregnant with her 4th child and that Allman had allegedly raped her. Police apparently discovered Allman had tried to use one of Hart's credit cards and that's how they ended up linking him to the crime.

On July 10th, 2012, Allman pleaded not guilty. He's charged with murder, robbery, rape, and fetal homicide. Prosecutors have said they plan to seek the death penalty when Allman is tried. The jury trial was originally scheduled for July 2013 then it was pushed back to October. Now it is on the docket for April 2014. Relatives say they want the death penalty sought and will not accept a guilty plea.

Ever since the tragedy, I've developed a close relationship with Hart's father, Wendell Roberts. Roberts has become more than just a news contact. Because he's a minister, I consider him a brother in the Lord. About the same time all of this was taking place, I was heading up the pulpit committee that was looking for a senior minister for the church I was attending and Wendell made it a point to offer some advice and to ask me how the hunt was going whenever we would talk. I was amazed by this man. Here was a father who had lost his daughter in about the worst way possible and his faith was as strong as ever. Yet he did tell me about his worlds "colliding" after one court appearance in September 2012.

"Because we have anger on one hand, and then we want to offer forgiveness on the other," Roberts told me.

And I was about to learn another great example of triumph in time of tragedy.

In August 2012, the first annual "Run With All Your Hart" took place. Hart was a pharmacist and her family wanted to give other young people a way to advance careers in that field. So they scheduled a run with proceeds going towards scholarships for teens wanting to pursue careers in the pharmaceutical area. $70,000 was raised from the first event. It was enough to provide scholarships to four people. Four people that had it not been for the RWAYH would have had to look elsewhere for their higher education funds.

"She is being remembered, every time you turn around," Roberts said.

"We're not thinking about the suspect, we are focusing on Sarah and her life and family and trying to get past that and on to the healing process," race organizer Stephanie Foley told me during a story previewing the run on July 10$^{th}$, 2012.

A year later the second annual event was held and I was able to interview Hart's sister, Elizabeth.

"And I think when tragedies hit, God is good even in tragedy. God will bring good in the long run," she said.

At both events, thousands participated. And in the first year, hundreds took part in virtual races in their hometowns with pictures showing up on Facebook of people with their Run With All Your Hart shirts in towns all over the United States and even beyond America's borders.

"It is something I think Sarah would want us to do. She would have loved helping people pursue something people would have had difficulty doing," Elizabeth Roberts told me in an August 6, 2013 story.

## Kinney Noe's Miracle.

Sometimes what starts out as a tragedy or what you think is going to be a tragedy turns out to be so incredible the only way you can describe it is to call it miraculous. And Kinney Noe of Stanford is one example of just that.

On November 13, 2011, Noe and his daughter were hunting on his property in rural Lincoln County near the Ottenheim community. Noe was 25 feet up in a tree stand. Something went wrong and he fell, right on top of a branch that impaled him.

"Up through my abdomen, colon, up to my liver and my diaphragm," Noe would later tell me of the three-inch-thick branch that entered his body at his waist and exited near his neck. Noe will tell you himself, he should have died. A year later, Noe told me his entire story in what was his first media interview.

He said the first miracle was that he survived the fall, the second was that he was able to call his daughter for help with his cell phone in an area where reception is usually non-existent.

EMS workers arrived and still able to talk, he feared he was about to breathe his last.

"And I said, do me a favor. Call my wife and tell her I love her and the girls very much. If I don't make it through," Noe told me of his conversation with the medic on the air ambulance.

Noe was loaded onto the helicopter and rushed to the University of Kentucky trauma center. He credits paramedic Aaron Stamper of Stanford in making the crucial decision to leave the branch in him until they arrived at UK. When he arrived he had no blood pressure. He would stay there for 169 days in and out of comas and consciousness. His wife, Rita, rarely left his side.

When he finally left the hospital, she cleaned out his wound every two hours even at night.

"There was never any time that I said 'I can't do this.' But I had that inner strength," she told me during an interview that aired on WKYT on Nov. 1, 2012. She said it was another miracle that for one year, she never fell ill, never even suffered a cold, and somehow got through each day with very little sleep or rest.

"She has been with me since day one. And has been there for everything," Kinney said.

Noe says it took nearly a year to completely heal from the injury and says he still feels pain from it. But he says all of it has made him a better person.

"And I give all the praise to my Lord and Savior Jesus Christ. And it's turned my life around. Made me re-dedicate my life to the Lord," Noe said.

Since then Noe has told this story to numerous churches and organizations. It's yet one more example of something bad happening, and the good that comes from it. And a story I've been able to tell.

The Jaden Jasper Miracle.

If Kinney Noe was the Lincoln County miracle, then what happened to 12-year-old Jaden Jasper in March 2013 was the Pulaski County miracle.

On March 5th, Jimmy Jasper picked up his daughter from volleyball practice at Northern Middle School in Somerset. On the way home, Jimmy's SUV lost control on Pumphouse Road, ran off the road and crashed through a wooden fence. Several of the planks from that fence came into the truck, impaling both Jimmy and his daughter. Both were rushed to UK and relatives would later tell me they feared Jaden would not survive. Jimmy was treated for several days and released. Jaden's treatment would take much longer.

"This morning they have inserted a lumbar drain because she was having spinal fluid that was building up," her uncle, Doug Miller told me the day after the crash.

The day after the accident one of Jaden's middle school classmates and her sister took it upon themselves to start up a Facebook page called "Prayers for Jaden." It quickly caught on and within hours hundreds of people "liked" the page. Those numbers soon became thousands and people just didn't answer the call to pray, they answered the call to donate money.

Soon t-shirts with the "pray for Jaden" slogan were made up and sold. Bake sales, benefit concerts, chili suppers, you name it, it happened. And everything went for Jaden's recovery.

"It has been a very overwhelming thing the amount of people that have wanted to help the family," Rev. Tony Hall of Barnesburg Baptist Church told me on March 12, 2013,

Jaden's injuries were very severe. Because of the way the wooden planks hit her in the head, she underwent major surgeries. But even in the weeks right after the crash, people were amazed by her recovery.

"She has opened her right eye, she is responding by shaking her head yes and no and she's given a thumbs up and moving her fingers," Rev. Hall told me.

A few months later, despite Jaden's incredible recovery, there was more bad news. Blood work on Mr. Jasper came back showing he was allegedly drunk when the crash happened and he was arrested and charged with assault. He pleaded guilty to those charges on July 19th, 2013.

"I was driving drunk and ran off the road and caused serious injury to my daughter," Jasper told Hon. David Tapp during the court proceeding. Jasper said that before the crash, he had taken sleeping pills, anxiety meds and topped all of that off with 12 beers.

Jasper was sentenced to ten years in prison but because of what Jaden herself asked of prosecutors, he was not incarcerated any more.

"Her wishes very strongly to me where 'don't put my Daddy in jail,'" Commonwealth's Attorney Eddy Montgomery told the judge as Mr. Jasper stood before the bench.

Jasper was ordered to be on home incarceration and probation for five years. Any violation of random drug or alcohol tests or if some other violation seen during a home visit could land him behind bars to serve the entire decade-long sentence.

"If he makes any mistake, I will be asking this judge to revoke his probation. Our judges are very strict on probation," Montgomery told me after the proceeding.

On September 9th, Jaden gave her first and only media interview. I was fortunate enough to develop a close relationship with her family and was granted the exclusive, one time interview with this amazing survival story. Jaden talked about her accident and recovery in the days after the family that helped her, suffered their own tragedy.

On September 6th when driving home from work, Joe Phillippi, 37, was killed when his car collided with a tractor trailer. Joe's daughters were the ones that started the popular "Prayers for Jaden" Facebook page. Jaden's family wanted to help the Phillippi family so they started a "Prayers for the Phillippi Family" page. Jaden herself had a role in that page.

"I understand what they're going through," Jaden told me in the September 9th story. "The biggest part was that people loved me, and it helped me get stronger."

Jaden's aunt, Karen, told me she firmly believed the call to pray for her niece in the Facebook page was the sole reason she survived both the accident and got through the months of recovery.

"I felt so great that so many people cared so much to pray that hard for me and my dad. That's the reason I'm sitting here, was because of that, and I think them for that," Jaden told me.

# EPILOGUE

Well, that's about it so far. On November 10, 2013 I celebrated my 10-year anniversary with WKYT. I must admit that when I was working in radio in the 1990s I had no idea that one day I would work in television news, much less work in it as long as I have. I have been blessed and I am very fortunate to do what I do.

I still find it humorous, though when I'm set up, doing my stand-ups and someone will drive by, usually honk, and yell out, "Hey, can't they afford to get you a photographer!" Or sometimes it's "Aren't you good enough for your own video guy?!"

The truth is, I like it the way it is. Sure, there are times I appreciate help and there are some stories you have to have a videographer to assist you with. Such was the case when Kenny Harvener and I went to Washington, D.C. in 2005 to cover the 10 Commandments case. But the truth be told, I simply love being a "one man band" (or multi media journalist) and everything that comes with it.

The last few stories I talked about here have a common theme of good happening amidst tragedy. And that's another thing that makes this job so rewarding. Yes, it's true that most of the news is bad. Tragedy happens. And research may show that viewers do watch bad news more or pay attention to it more than the "good" news. But the worst of times do bring out the best in some. Sometimes it brings out the worst in others, and that too makes the news. But everything I have written here I hope leaves you with some hope. Some hope that despite everything that is wrong with our world, that despite evil things taking place, we can have hope. We have hope in God. I'm a Christian and I'm not ashamed of my relationship with Jesus.

Sure I've made mistakes. I even remember getting an email or a message one time after I had reported on something (I don't remember what the story was) and the emailer or caller simply asked "how can you sleep at night?"

Sometimes this job puts us in situations we would rather not be in. But I have come to know and believe it's not what happens to us, it's how we react to what happens to us. That truly sets us apart and I hope how I have reacted to everything life has given me has been to do what is right. Thanks for reading and God Bless you!

WKYT
27 NEWSFIRST

GO BIG BLUE!

WKYT
27 NEWSFIRST

NEWSROOM at
THE CENTER

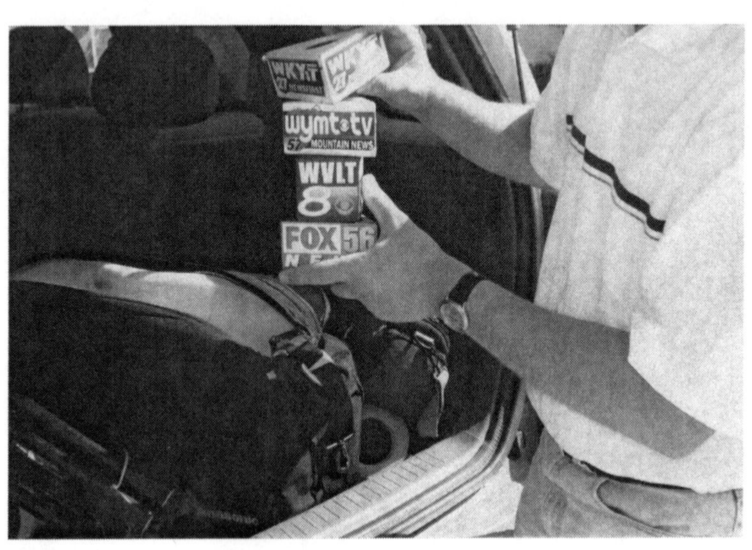
WKYT
wymt tv
MOUNTAIN NEWS
WVLT
8
FOX 56

WKYT
27
NEWSFIRST

CPSIA information can be obtained at www.ICGtesting.com
Printed in the USA
LVOW11s0245170614

390288LV00001B/60/P